BEFORE REVIVAL BEGINS

THE PREACHER'S PREPARATION FOR A REVIVAL MEETING

Compiled and Edited by
Dan R. Crawford

Introduction by
Dr. Ken Hemphill, President
Southwestern Baptist Theological Seminary

1996

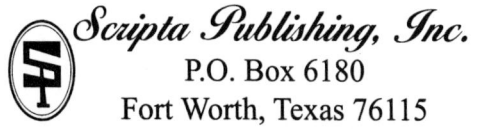

Scripta Publishing, Inc.
P.O. Box 6180
Fort Worth, Texas 76115

BEFORE REVIVAL BEGINS

Copyright © 1996 by Dan R. Crawford

All rights reserved. No portion of this book may be reproduced in any form, except for brief quotations in reviews, without written permission from the publisher.

Library of Congress Cataloging-in-Publication Data

Crawford, Dan R.
    Before revival begins: the preacher's preparation for a revival meeting /Dan R. Crawford
        p. cm.
    Bibliography: p.
        ISBN 1-889730-01-7
    1. Christianity—Evangelism. 2. Biblical—Evangelism. I. Title. 1996

Printed in the United States of America

This book is dedicated to the thousands of students who, since 1958, have participated in Southwestern Baptist Seminary's Pioneer Penetration/Operation Penetration/Spring Evangelism Practicum and to the thousands who will participate in the future.

Special thanks to the 16 "Southwesterners" who contributed to this book without personal, financial remuneration.

Contents

Introduction vii
Ken Hemphill

Part One
Personal Preparation for a Revival Meeting

Preparing Spiritually for a Revival Meeting 1
Dan Crawford

Preparing by Studying
the History of Revival Meetings 17
Alvin Reid

Preparing Sermons Through Bible Study 27
James Heflin

Preparing Sermons for a Revival Meeting 37
Malcolm McDow

Preparing Sermon Illustrations
for a Revival Meeting 51
Endel Lee

Preparing to Communicate
the Message in a Revival Meeting 65
Al Fasol

Preparing to Reach the Lost 73
Robert Naylor

Preparing for a Revival Meeting
by Becoming a Servant in the Pulpit 83
Calvin Miller

Preparing for Invitations in a Revival Meeting 91
Roy Fish

Preparing for a Revival Meeting in
a Multi-congregational Church 103
Ebbie Smith

Preparing for a Revival Meeting
in an Hispanic Church 111
Daniel Sanchez

Preparing for a Revival Meeting in a Black Church 123
Raymond Spencer

Preparing to Minister To and With the Pastor 131
Jimmie Nelson

Preparing for People of Other Persuasions 137
Thomas Wright

Preparing to Witness to Strangers 155
Jimmy Sharp

PART TWO
Model Revival Sermons Blessed by God

Certainty For An Uncertain World 171
Roy Fish

Life's Supreme Question 179
Malcolm McDow

With Time on Our Minds 187
Dan Crawford

Five Steps to Servanthood 195
Calvin Miller

The Missing Component 203
Ken Hemphill

Revival Bibliography 211

Introduction

The Revival Meeting: Help or Hindrance?

As you consider this book, you may first be pondering this question: *Is the revival meeting a help or hindrance to church growth?* Is it a relic of past methodology or a God-given tool vital to the future of the church? Some of the materials written on church growth appear to give the impression that special meetings are archaic trappings of the past and can easily be discarded by the church of the twenty-first century.[1] Before we cast aside the revival meeting or special evangelistic meeting, I urge you to take a more balanced look.

A Look at Potential Results

First, all authentic church growth is supernatural by definition. When Jesus founded the church, He promised that He would build it (Matt. 16:18). Thus the first step in church growth is a supernatural encounter or awakening. The "revival meeting" has often been used by God to provide this supernatural ignition in the life of an otherwise dormant church.

Second, some "revival meetings" have been used of God for an evangelistic harvest. It appears to me some have been uniquely gifted to draw the net in terms of evangelistic decisions. The Apostle Paul mentions the gift of the evangelist in Ephesians 4:11 in the same context as his mention of pastor/teacher. I can see no evidence that the exalted Christ's gift to His church of evangelists has been revoked. If anything, in our day of growing secularity, the gift is in greater demand than ever before.

Third, a "revival meeting" often creates a climate for evangelism in the life of the host church. Most church growth authors agree that evangelistic results are often connected to a passionate concern for the lost, love for the Lord, His church and His people, and a spirit of excitement and expectancy. A "revival meeting" will often help to produce such a climate by making the church aware of the need of the lost and their own lack of evangelistic activity. In his book, *A New Day in Church Revivals*, Bill Cathey says:

> To this day about 75 percent of evangelistic churches schedule one or more revival meetings annually . . . Some pastors and churches have become disillusioned with revival meetings and have abandoned them. Others have cut back on revival meetings. Some have gone to four-day mini-revivals and week-end revivals. Still others have substituted deeper life conferences, Bible conferences, family life conferences, and such. Though all of these are good, when they take the place of revival meetings, the end result is fewer professions of faith.[2]

Using the Tool

I tend to be a collector of tools even though I rarely learn how to use them. Many of my tools do not accomplish their designed task but the problem lies not in the tool but the user. The current day criticism and disdain for the "revival meeting" tool tells us more about our inability to use the tool than the tool's ability to accomplish its task. Writing on the current use of the revival meeting, Charles Kelly of New Orleans Baptist Seminary concludes, "For the foreseeable future, it will be a viable tool for evangelism . . . Many churches find them to be the most productive tool they use in evangelism."[3]

One of the key factors of the successful revival meeting is preparation. C. E. Matthews argued that preparation is 75% of the success of the revival crusade. Thorough preparation involves both the spiritual and the organizational. These must be intentionally balanced. There is an issue that is prior to the preparation of the church and that is the preparation of the preacher. This book fits that critical and unique niche of preparing the preacher for the revival meeting. It is an essential textbook that you will want to use over and over again in your revival meeting preparation.

Endnotes

1. An excellent study conducted recently demonstrates the continuing popularity and effectiveness of revival meetings among Southern Baptist churches. Ronald Wayne Johnson, *An Evaluation of the Home Mission Board Programs of Evangelism in Local Churches*, unpublished D.Min. thesis, The Southern Baptist Theological Seminary, 1988.

2. Bill V. Cathey, *A New Day in Church Revivals*, (Nashville: Broadman Press, 1984), 5-6.

Ken S. Hemphill is President of Southwestern Baptist Theological Seminary in Fort Worth, Texas and also serves as Professor of Evangelism and Church Growth.

Part One

Personal Preparation for a Revival Meeting

Preparing Spiritually for a Revival Meeting

Having been thrilled at the sound of his own introduction, the young minister walked confidently to the pulpit to begin his sermon. As the sermon developed (or perhaps "deteriorated" would be a more descriptive word) the preacher's confidence gave way to frustration and ultimately to despair. Struggling with words and phrases, the novice had almost reached the point of panic when he found his conclusion. When he had completed his sermon, the dejected preacher walked from the pulpit with his head hung low and his spirit crushed. Following the service, an older, wiser minister put his arm around the young learner and counseled him with the advice; "Young man, if you had gone into the pulpit like you came out, you could have come out like you went in." Misplaced confidence had offered one young preacher both a miserable evening and a valuable lesson. Lack of proper spiritual preparation will always hinder the preacher. Let's look at four biblical means of spiritual preparation that will, if followed, prevent the previous story from being your experience.

First, a definition of corporate and personal revival. Richard Owen Roberts defines revival as, "an extraordinary movement of the Holy Spirit producing extraordinary results."[1] When applied to the personal, this means an extraordinary movement of the Holy Spirit in your life. How long has it been since you experienced an extraordinary movement of God's Spirit in your life? A movement in which God's Spirit comes down and God's Word comes home and God's purity comes through and God's preacher comes alive.[2] When this happens, there will be extraordinary results, but we must remember, there is a difference in genuine revival and revival meetings.

> Revival meetings are worked up;
> Revival is prayed down,
> Revival meetings are something the church decides to do for God;
> Revival is something God decides to do for the church.
> Revival meetings are accompanied by songs and sermons;
> Revival is accompanied by signs and wonders.
> In revival meetings man takes the initiative;
> In revival God takes the initiative.
> In revival meetings the message of the Holy One is lifted up;
> In revival the Spirit of the Holy One comes down.
> In revival meetings the community calendar takes its toll;
> In revival the Holy Spirit takes control.
> In revival meetings, "mercy drops 'round us are falling";
> In revival, "showers of blessing we'll see".
> In revival meetings we are often recipients of blessing;
> In revival we become channels of blessing.
> In revival meetings the offering is raised;
> In revival the fire falls.
> In revival meetings we say, "how many must we attend?";
> In revival we say, "Hallelujah, thine the glory, revive us again";
> In revival meetings we sing, "He is Lord";
> In revival, He is Lord!

Leonard Ravenhill said, genuine revival, "cannot be organized . . . subsidized . . . advertised . . . computerized . . . regularized . . . rationalized . . . denominationalized . . . or nationalized."[3] There is a real difference between revival and revival meetings. God has given us a formula of preparation by which the Spirit can produce extraordinary revival in and through us. The first step is

The Preparation of Brokenness

The preacher for a revival meeting must be humbled before God, before God will send revival to and through him. Often God brings the preacher to the point of brokenness so that he may be used more effectively as an instrument of revival.

The founder of Southwestern Baptist Seminary, B.H. Carroll, was preaching a revival meeting in Belton, Texas when he became distraught over the lack of response. After several sleepless nights, Carroll got up one night, dressed, and went walking. He walked all the way to the town's cemetery. There he fell on his knees and in brokenness, prayed, "Lord, if you have called me to preach, I want you to show me what Hell is like." That night, God responded to the broken, humbled preacher and revealed to him the horrible destiny of the lost. The next evening Carroll preached with such intensity that those present said it seemed as though flames of fire were leaping in his face. God revived the broken preacher, then sent revival through him.

Now, there is a difference in being broken and being crushed. Stones are chipped and shaped to fit the purpose of the artist. Those stones that resist are crushed and destroyed. Being broken means to be obedient, not resistant to God's shaping of our lives. Charles G. Finney said, "a revival is nothing else than a new beginning of obedience to God . . . a deep repentance, a breaking down of heart, a getting down into the dust before God, with deep humility, and a forsaking of sin."[4] How then shall we humble ourselves? How shall we be broken? Only by placing ourselves up against the standard of God's Word will we be broken and humbled. Pray the prayer of the Psalmist, "Search me, O God, and know my heart; Try me, and know my anxieties; and see if there be any wicked way in me, and lead me in the way everlasting" (Ps. 139:23-24 NKJV). The following pretest for personal revival may be helpful as you seek to humble yourself and be broken. Be honest with yourself as you answer each question. Agree with God about each need revealed in your life. Confess each sin, with the willingness to make it right and forsake it. Praise God for being forgiving and correcting. Renew your mind and rebuild your life through meditation on and practical application of the Word of God. Review these questions periodically to remain sensitive to your need for ongoing revival.[5]

1. Genuine Salvation (II Corinthians 5:17)
   a. Was there ever a time in my life that I placed all my trust in Jesus Christ alone to save me?
   b. Was there ever a time in my life that I completely surrendered to Jesus Christ as the Master and Lord of my life?
2. God's Word (Psalm 119:97, 140)
   a. Do I love to read and meditate on the Word of God?
   b. Are my personal devotions consistent and meaningful?
3. Humility (Isaiah 57:15)
   a. Am I quick to recognize and confess when I have sinned?
   b. Do I rejoice when others are praised and recognized and my accomplishments go unnoticed by men?
4. Obedience (Hebrews 13:17; I Samuel 15:22)
   a. Do I consistently obey what I know God wants me to do?
   b. Do I consistently obey the human authorities over my life?
5. Pure Heart (I John 1:9)
   a. Do I confess my sin by name?
   b. Do I keep "short sin accounts" with God (confess and forsake as God convicts)?
6. Clear Conscience (Acts 24:16)
   a. Do I consistently seek forgiveness from those I wrong or offend?
   b. Is my conscience clear with every person?
7. Priorities (Matthew 6:33)
   a. Does my schedule reveal that God is first in my life?
   b. Does my checkbook reveal that God is first in my life?
8. Values (Colossians 3:12)
   a. Do I value highly the things that please God?
   b. Are my affections and goals fixed on eternal values?
9. Sacrifice (Philippians 3:7-11)
   a. Am I willing to sacrifice whatever is necessary to see God active in my life and church?
   b. Is my life characterized by genuine sacrifice for the cause of Christ?

10. Spirit Control (Galatians 5:22-25; Ephesians 5:18-21)
    a. Am I allowing the Holy Spirit to "fill" (control) my life each day?
    b. Is there consistent evidence of the "Fruit of the Spirit" being produced in my life?

11. "First Love" (Philippians 1:21-26)
    a. Am I as much in love with Jesus as I have ever been?
    b. Am I thrilled with Jesus, filled with His joy and peace, and making Him the continual object of my love?

12. Motives (Acts 5:29; Matthew 10:28)
    a. Would I pray, read my Bible, give, and serve as much if nobody but God ever noticed?
    b. Am I more concerned about pleasing God than I am about being accepted and appreciated by others?

13. Moral Purity (Ephesians 5:3-4)
    a. Do I keep my mind free from that which stimulates thoughts that are not morally pure?
    b. Are my conversation and behavior pure and above reproach?

14. Forgiveness (Colossians 3:12-13)
    a. Do I seek to resolve conflicts in relationships as soon as possible?
    b. Am I quick to forgive those who wrong me or hurt me?

15. Sensitivity (Matthew 5:23-24)
    a. Am I sensitive to the convictions and promptings of God's Spirit?
    b. Am I quick to respond in humility and obedience to the conviction and promptings of God's Spirit?

16. Evangelism (Romans 9:3; Luke 24:46, 48)
    a. Do I have a burden for the unsaved?
    b. Do I consistently witness for Christ?

17. Prayer (I Timothy 2:1)
    a. Am I faithful in praying for the needs of others?
    b. Do I pray specifically, fervently, and faithfully for revival in my life, my church, and my world?

Brokenness comes with God's judgement and just as judgement must, "begin at the house of God" it, "begins with us first" (I Peter 4:17 NKJV). There is a popular saying, "If it isn't broken, don't fix it!" In terms of personal revival, if it isn't broken, God won't fix it. The preparation of brokenness must be accompanied by

The Preparation of Prayerfulness

Just as, "the awakenings that have blessed the church in days gone by have usually come in response to the cries of a praying remnant,"[6] so your personal revival must be preceded by prayer.

Beginning in September of 1857 and extending into the spring of 1858 more than 250,000 people were saved and it all began in a prayer meeting. A businessman by the name of Jeremiah Lanphier announced a prayer meeting for layman to be held in the North Dutch Reformed Church at the corner of Fulton and William Streets in New York City at noon on Wednesday, September 23, 1857. While only a few men participated on the first Wednesday, soon every room in the church was filled, not just on Wednesday but five days a week at noon. Then other churches became filled with praying men. The great Prayer Revival crossed into Brooklyn, then down the eastern seaboard, and across the mountain ranges back toward the west. Miraculous, extraordinary accounts of revival were told and it began in a prayer meeting.

Our forefathers, at "protracted meetings" used to pray till the "break" came, then stand back and watch as God sent revival. They had time to wait and pray and so must you. William Carey preached, "the first, and most important of those duties which are incumbent upon us (in the task of advancing Christ's kingdom across the face of the earth), is fervent and united prayer."[7]

You must pray for personal revival. The brevity of time spent in the actual revival meeting allows you no time for a spiritual "warm-up" after you arrive on the field. The spirit must be right before the first service begins. While you have little or no control over the spiritual preparation of the church where the revival meeting is to be held, you do have some control of your own spiritual preparation and prayer is the prime means of that preparation. With the privilege of preaching a revival meeting comes the awesome responsibility of being spiritually prepared. Listen to Andrew Murray:

The prayer for revival is a most heart-searching thing. With it comes tremendous responsibilities. It needs great divine grace. It asks if we are ready to turn our hearts and lives from other interests and to bear the weight and sorrow of those in the city of God who sigh and cry because of the abominations that are done in the midst thereof. It asks if we so believe in prayer—in our right and power with God to undertake this great request—that God shall entirely change the life of some, of many, of His people form one of selfishness to one of entire self-sacrifice. It asks whether we will be the first to give the answer, to offer ourselves for the Holy Spirit to do His full work of convincing of sin and consuming what is of self. It asks if we will accept and carry the answer to our brethren and prove what God can do. Oh, this prayer for revival may mean much to us in more ways than one, but let us not fear. Let us unhesitatingly bring the whole tithe into His house; let us unhesitatingly expect to see the windows of heaven opened and floods of blessing poured out.[8]

You must likewise pray for your times of personal witness during the revival meeting. Pray that God will give you boldness in your witness remembering that the word, "boldness" contains not only the aggressiveness of presentation, but he clearness of expression.

Not only does the Bible instruct us to pray related to personal witness, it gives us many specific areas in which to pray. Pray that the Holy Spirit would draw the non-Christian to God (John 6:44). Pray the that non-believer would seek to know God (Acts 17:27; Deut. 4:29). Pray that the non-believer would believe the scriptures to be true and accurate (I Thes. 2:13; Rom. 10:17). Pray that Satan would be bound from blinding the eyes of the non-believer to the truth (Matt. 13:19; II Cor. 4:4). Pray that the Holy Spirit would work in the life of the non-believer (John 16:8-13). Pray that God would send someone who would show the non-believer the way to faith in Christ (Matt. 9:37-38). Pray that the non-believer would believe in Jesus Christ as his Lord and Savior (John 1:12; 5:24). Pray that the non-believer would turn away from sin (Acts 17:30-31, 3:19). Pray that the non-believer would confess Jesus Christ as Lord (Rom. 10:9-10). Pray that the non-believer would yield everything in order to follow Jesus Christ (II Cor. 5:15; Phil. 3:7-8). Finally, pray that the non-believer would take root and grow in Christ (Col. 2:6-7).[9]

Pray for personal revival. Pray for personal witness. And pray for public proclamation. Sermon preparation for a revival meeting must begin in prayer. Here is the principle: Never talk to the people about God until you've talked to God about the people. Robert E. Coleman says, "the place to begin in sermon preparation is on our knees."[10]

You should seek God's guidance as to the scripture passages and title through prayer. You will have the experience of someone saying to you following a sermon, "You could not have known how much I needed that sermon" and they will be right. But God knew and revealed it to you in prayer as you sought a text and topic. Saturate with prayer, your study of the passage on which you are to speak. While prayer is no substitute for study, neither is study a substitute for prayer. Then pray before and during your presentation of the sermon. God's anointing is available to every preacher for a price—and the price is prayer.

Having offered a through, thrilling and helpful presentation of the history of the Concerts of Prayer beginning with Jonathan Edwards, Robert Bakke comes to the conclusion of his book with these words, "pastors and ministry leaders should recognize the enormous value of establishing a rhythm of prayer for the revival of the church and the advancement of Christ's kingdom."[11] The preparations of brokenness and prayerfulness must be joined by

The Preparation of Holiness

In his excellent book, *Revival: A People Saturated with God,* Brian Edwards says:

> The men God uses in revival all have a burning conviction that God will not hold back from giving "good things" to his people and so they have a bold impertinence to ask and expect good things from him. But they are equally sure that these are only given to "those whose walk is blameless" (Psalm 84:11). They know that sin will quench the Holy Spirit, and their passion for God is equalled only by their fear of offending him. These are not men who take God lightly. Their understanding of the holy character of their Creator is awful in its scope.[12]

In 1734, four years prior to his conversion, John Wesley declared, "My one aim in life is to secure personal holiness, for without being holy myself I cannot promote real holiness in others"[13] and neither can you. Before God will use you as an instrument in revival, you must be holy. Prior to every significant revival in Christian history there has been a deep desire on the part of some, for a return to holiness. It must begin in you.

R.A. Torrey was said to have had what he called, "A Prescription for Revival" which proposed:

(1) Let a few Christians get thoroughly right with God themselves.

(2) Let them bind themselves together to pray for revival till God opens the heavens and comes down.

(3) Let them put themselves at the disposal of God to use them as he sees fit in winning others to Christ.

The "Prescription" begins with holiness ("right with God") and that's where your prescription must likewise begin.

Isaiah prophesied concerning a highway of holiness:

> A highway will be there, and a road,
> And it shall be called the Highway of Holiness.
> The unclean shall not pass over it.
> But it shall be for others. Whoever walks the road,
> Although a fool, shall not go astray.
> No lion shall be there,
> Nor shall any ravenous beast go up on it;
> It shall not be found there.
> But the redeemed shall walk there,
> And the ransomed of the Lord shall return,
> And come to Zion with singing,
> With everlasting joy on their heads.
> They shall obtain joy and gladness,
> And sorrow and sighing shall flee away.
>
> Isaiah 35:8-10 (NKJV)

Likewise, the New Testament is filled with calls to personal holiness:

(1) "Behold, I send you out as sheep in the midst of wolves. Therefore, be wise as serpents and harmless as doves." Matthew 10:16 (NKJV)

(2) "I want you to be wise in what is good, and simple concerning evil." Romans 16:19b (KNJV)

(3) "Brethren, do not be children in understanding; however, in malice be babes, but in understanding be mature." I Cor. 14:20 (NKJV)

(4) "Therefore, 'come out from among them and be separate', says the Lord." II Cor. 6:17 (NKJV)

(5) "But fornication and all uncleanness or covetousness, let it not even be named among you, as is fitting for saints." Eph. 5:3 (NKJV)

(6) "Finally, brethren, whatever things are true, whatever things are noble, whatever things are just, whatever things are pure, whatever things are lovely, whatever things are of good report, if there be any virtue and if there is anything praiseworthy—meditate on these things." Phil 4:8 (NKJV)

(7) "Set your minds on things above, not on things on the earth." Col. 3:2 (NKJV)

(8) "Pure and undefiled religion before God and the Father is this: to visit orphans and widows in their trouble, and to keep oneself unspotted from the world." James 1:27 (NKJV)

(9) "Hating even the garment defiled by the flesh." Jude 23b (NKJV)

One of the ways the Bible instructs us to holiness is by encouraging us to seek God's face. The Psalmist says, "Seek the Lord and His strength; Seek His face evermore." (Ps. 105:4 NKJV) Then the Psalmist asks, "When shall I come and behold the face of God?" (Ps. 42:2 RSV). In regard to a revival meeting, you should behold the face of God in preparation. Seek God's face in personal devotion, in prayer, in sermon preparation, in invitation planning, in daily routine, in family life, in travel arrangements, in interpersonal relationships, in correspondence, in all of life.

The preparation of brokenness, prayerfulness and holiness, must be complimented by

The Preparation of Sinlessness

Prior to every great movement of God, the world has been marked by gross sinfulness. When Satan runs rampant on the earth, God begins to look for those who in bad times seek to remain good, those who in godless days seek to remain God fearing, those who in careless days seek to remain constant in purity, those who in earthy days seek to have eternity in their hearts, those who in sinful days seek to remain undefeated by sin. The sinfulness of man, the lawlessness in the world, the permissiveness of society are not indications that revival is impossible. They are rather, indications that revival is imperative and if history is to be repeated, inevitable. Flee, therefore, form sin, that you might be one whom God chooses to use in revival.

The beginning of the eighteenth century was a time of material prosperity and wide-spread sinfulness in England. While colonies poured new wealth into the mother country, luxury, dishonesty, speculation and extravagance reigned supreme. It was a time of increased intellectual activity and expression. The freedom of worship secured during the Reformation had degenerated to the point that all authority, human and divine, was defied. Hobbs and Locke increased the popularity of infidelity. Gibbon and Hume were busy discrediting the church. In a spiritual chill, the church seemed helpless. The ministry became increasingly corrupt. The Sabbath was just another day and God was openly defied. Just when the outlook seemed its darkest, God invaded history once again. In 1703, three men were born, John Wesley in England, Gilbert Tennent in Ireland and Jonathan Edwards in Massachusetts. These three, along with the George Whitefield (born eleven years later) would become the human instruments of the great spiritual awakening that swept over England and America in just a few years. God had raised up men who hated sin in the midst of a sin-crazed world and God is again looking for such who will, "turn from their wicked ways" and be used.

Ask God to use the following questions to help you identify the degree to which your attitude toward God is one of repentance from sin:[14]

(1) Do I have a heart attitude that says, "Lord, everything I now know to be sin, and everything You show me in the future to be sin, I am willing to give it all up for Your sake"?

(2) Have I ever experienced the repentance that characterizes genuine salvation? Was my "conversion" experience mere external reformation, rather than internal heart transformation?

(3) Can I truly say that I am willing to forsake every sin in my life, including those which are not known to others?

(4) Am I willing to call my wrongful acts sins, rather than characterizing them as weaknesses, flaws, or personality traits?

(5) Am I more grieved over how my sin has offended a holy God (repentance), than I am over the consequences that I have reaped for my sin (remorse)?

(6) Am I willing to accept personal responsibility for my actions, without pointing the finger of blame at anyone else?

(7) Am I willing to take whatever steps may be necessary to make complete restitution for my sin?

(8) Am I willing, if necessary, to confess my sin publicly before men, as well as privately before God?

(9) Am I willing to face the possible consequences of public repentance, such as loss of reputation, position, or influence?

(10) Am I willing, if necessary, to suffer the loss of all things in exchange for being clean before both God and man?

(11) Am I willing to voluntarily yield privileges and positions of leadership to demonstrate a repentant spirit?

(12) Am I willing to submit to the disciplines of man for my sin, as well as those consequences directly imposed by God?

(13) Am I willing to be accountable to another believer in those areas of my life where I have experienced past failure, in order that I may develop new patterns of victory?

(14) Have I at any time in the past year experienced genuine repentance, resulting in a change of actions, attitudes, and spirit? At any time since my conversion? Can I specifically illustrate repentance out of my life?

(15) Am I willing to testify openly concerning where God found me before I repented?

(16) Are there any specific sins in my life that I have never truly repented of? Am I willing to repent of those sins here and now? (Why not take time right now to list those sins on a separate piece of paper, and to confess them with the intent to forsake them? As you do, exercise faith in the power of God to set you free from every sinful bondage.

Once you have repented of the "big sins" in your life, don't forget the lilywork. When Solomon's Temple was constructed, the materials were of immense value. Cedar and cyprus trunks were cut in the high mountains and floated on huge rafts down the river to Joppa, then 35 miles *up* to Jerusalem. The construction took 7 years, with the help of 30,000 Israelites and 150,000 Canaanites, and was completed without the sound of a hammer or the use of tools. Two bronze pillars sat near the porch. On top of these pillars—27 feet high—where no human eye could see the details was the lilywork. The Bible says, "Upon the top of the pillars was lilywork" (I Kings 7:22 KJV). The workers had given great care to that which was only to be seen by God.

"Do you not know that your body is the temple of the Holy Spirit who is in you? (I Cor. 6:19 NKJV) Take care of the unseen, unknown, minute details of your life—the lilywork—that which is so hidden only God can see it. Your preparation is incomplete until you've dealt with the lilywork of your life.

Conclusion

That's God's formula for personal revival meeting preparation. Now, you ask, is it biblical? Good question: When God appeared to Solomon in response to Solomon's prayer, God made a promise with four prerequisite conditions. These conditions—and the promise—are still good. God said, "If my people, which are called by me name, shall humble themselves (The Preparation of Brokenness), and pray (The Preparation of Prayerfulness), and seek my face (The Preparation of Holiness), and turn from their wicked ways (The Preparation of Sinlessness); then will I hear from heaven, and will forgive their sin, and will heal their land." (II Chron. 7:14 KJV).

While preaching an Easter revival meeting in Ngaruawahia, New Zealand in 1936, J. Edwin Orr was standing in line at the Post Office one afternoon contemplating his text for the evening, Psalm 139:23-24. In the background he heard some Maori girls singing one of their native songs, "The Song of Farewell". The first line, "Now is the hour when we must say goodbye" captured Orr's attention and in five minutes he had set the words of his text to the native tune, thus capturing the genius of personal revival meeting preparation:

> Search me, O God, and know my heart today;
> Try me, O Savior, know my thoughts, I pray.
> See if there be some wicked way in me;
> Cleanse me from ev'ry sin and set me free.
>
> I praise thee, Lord, for cleansing me from sin;
> Fulfill thy Word and make me pure within.
> Fill me with fire where once I burned with shame;
> Grant my desire to magnify thy name.
>
> Lord, take my life and make it wholy thine;
> Fill my poor heart with thy great love divine.

Take all my will, my passion, self, and pride:
I now surrender; Lord, in me abide.

O Holy Spirit, revival comes from thee;
Send a revival, start the work in me.
Thy Word declares Thou wilt supply our need;
For blessings now, O Lord, I humbly plead.

Endnotes

1. Richard Owen Roberts, *Revival* (Wheaton: Tyndale House Publishers, Inc., 1983), 16-17.

2. For a further treatment of this see *Keep in Step with the Spirit* by J.I. Packer (Old Tappan, NJ: Fleming H. Revell Co., 1984), pp. 244-245.

3. Leonard Ravenhill, *Revival God's Way* (Minneapolis: Bethany House Publishers, 1983), 64.

4. Charles G. Finney, *Finney On Revival:* The Highlights of the Sermons on Revival, Arranged by E.E. Shelharner (Minneapolis: Bethany House Publishers, N.D.), 9.

5. "Preparing for Personal Revival", *Spirit of Revival* (Buchanan, MI: Life Action Ministries, Vol. 18, Number 1) 37-39.

6. Arthur Wallis, *Revival: The Rain from Heaven* (Old Tappan, NJ: Power Books, Fleming H. Revell Co., 1979), 27.

7. William Carey, *An Enquiry into the Obligations of Christians, to Use Means for the Conversion of the Heathens* (Leicester, Printed and sold by Ann Ireland and Co., 1792; London, New Facsimile ed., 1961), 77.

8. Andrew Murray, *Revival* (Minneapolis: Bethany House Publishers, 1990). 15.

9. See also, *Connecting With God: The Priority of Communication in Prayer* by Dan R. Crawford (Fort Worth: Scripta Publishing Inc., 1994), pp. 86-87.

10. "Focusing the Message" by Robert E. Coleman, *Choose Ye This Day* (Minneapolis: World Wide Publication, 1989), 66.

11. Robert Bakke, *The Concert of Prayer: Back to the Future?* (Minneapolis: Evangelical Free Church of America, 1993), 147-148.

12. Brian H. Edwards, *Revival! A People Saturated With God* (Durham, England: Evangelical Press, 1990), 62.

13. Vulliamy, *John Wesley* (London: Geoffrey Bles, 1931), 60.

14. "Making it Personal" *Spirit of Revival* (Buchanan, MI: Life Action Ministries, Vol. 21, Number 3), 29-30.

Dan R. Crawford is Associate Professor of Evangelism and Missions and Director of Evangelism and Missions Practica at Southwestern Baptist Theological Seminary in Fort Worth, Texas. He is also occupant of the George W. Truett Chair of Ministry.

PREPARING BY STUDYING THE HISTORY OF REVIVAL MEETINGS

On March 19, 1995, several hundred students gathered for an evening service at Wheaton College in Illinois. That night two students from Howard Payne University in Brownwood, Texas, testified concerning a mighty movement of revival which spontaneously swept through the town and the university beginning in January.[15] After the two spoke, students by the dozens began to come forward, confessing sin, sharing burdens, and joining together in small groups to pray. At 6:00 A.M. there were more students in the chapel than when the service began! For the next four nights increasing numbers of students gathered to confess sin and to minister, until fifteen hundred gathered on March 23, for a celebration rally that lasted over five hours. Revival spread quickly from Howard Payne to over thirty schools across the nation.

Roy Hession once said that while prayer is the *foundation* for revival, testimony is its *fuel*. There is nothing more inspiring than a fresh, genuine testimony of the power of God in the life of a person, a church, or a college.

The accounts from the past great awakenings also can provide a stirring encouragement for the preacher of a revival meeting.

I discovered this personally when I was introduced to the stories of revival. After college graduation a pastor introduced me to the story of Rees Howells, a coal miner during the Welsh Revival.[16] My heart was broken over the things that kept me from experiencing a fresh touch from the Lord; at the same time, I was encouraged when I saw how God used Howells. A course on spiritual awakenings in seminary furthered my understanding of how God has worked in history. I began to think, if He did it then, He could do it now! Then, my doctoral studies focussed on the spiritual awakenings. Reading about how God used John Wesley, George Whitefield, Jonathan Edwards, and others pierced my heart. Oh, that God would do this in my lifetime! I have found that I am not alone in my yearnings to know more about revivals of the past. So, this chapter is an encouragement for you to study further about revivals.

Past Awakenings

Several notable movements have been documented as a testimony to the faithfulness of God in the past few centuries. These great awakenings generally followed a time of spiritual declension in the churches.

The First Great Awakening generally refers to the period of renewal in the early to mid-eighteenth century. This awakening was actually part of a larger movement which spread across the European continent and the British Isles.

The renewal movement known as Pietism influenced churches on the European continent. Pietism's origin is normally traced to Philip Spener's *Pia Desideria*, or "Pious Desires," published in 1675. This classic in Christian spirituality, was originally a manual of reform for Lutheran churches. Under the influence of Spener, Jean DeLabadie, Auguste H. Francke, and Count Nicolaus Von Zinzendorf among others, Pietism made a notable impact. Pietism emphasized personal devotion to God, a conversion experience, serious Bible study, and hymn singing.

Pietism had no small influence on leaders of the Great Awakening, including John Wesley in England and Theodore Frelinghuysen in America. The Evangelical Awakening in England (also called the Wesleyan Revival) centered on the impact of John and Charles Wesley with George Whitefield in Britain. The Methodist Church began out of this awakening. Some historians have argued that this awakening kept Britain from going through an event like the French Revolution.

It was Frelinghuysen who is credited by some as the catalyst of the earliest localized revivals in the colonies. This Dutch Reformed pastor in New Jersey emphasized regenerate church membership, zealous visitation, church discipline, and the use of *vorlessers* or lay helpers. The result was twofold as both revival and controversy began about 1726. William Tennent, a Presbyterian in Pennsylvania, taught his sons and other young men in a log cabin (dubbed "log college" by skeptics) Greek, logic, and other subjects while instilling a passion for evangelism. Several of the log college graduates experienced revival in their ministries. Gilbert Tennent was the best known son. The Presbyterian part of the revival led to controversy between the anti-revival Old Sides and Pro-Revival new sides. If your definition of revival omits the reality of opposition or persecution, study the history of the First Great Awakening!

Jonathan Edwards, one of the greatest intellects in American history, was a pivotal person in New England. Edwards pastored a significant Congregationalist church in Northhampton, Massachusetts. Revival came there at first in 1734-35. Edwards recorded the origins and extent of this awakening in his *Faithful Narrative*. The greatest outbreak of revival came in 1740-42. It was during this period that Edwards preached his famous sermon, "Sinners in the Hands of an Angry God," in a Connecticut church. Edwards' impact went far beyond his preaching. His writings are essential to any serious study of spiritual awakening.

Another example of the impact of this awakening can be seen in Baptist churches. In 1740, only twenty-one Baptist churches were in New England. In fifty years the number increased over one thousand percent to two hundred and sixty-six.[17]

George Whitefield, the itinerant orator from England who was part of the John Wesley's Holy Club at Oxford, came to the colonies on seven separate voyages. His preaching is credited with fanning the spark of revival into a raging flame. John Wesley and Whitefield led the awakening in England that resulted ultimately in the formation of the Methodist church.

The Second Great Awakening in America touched both colleges and churches in the east and the frontier to the west. Hampden-Sydney, Yale, and Williams colleges all reported powerful revivals from the last decade of the eighteenth century into the nineteenth. Timothy Dwight, grandson of Jonathan Edwards and president of Yale, was the spark to the revival at that school. At Williams College the "Haystack Prayer Meeting" occurred which led Samuel Mills to propose a mission to Asia. On the frontier the camp meetings erupted at the turn of the century. While led at first by Presbyterians such as James McGready, the Methodists ultimately gained the most from camp meetings. The most famous meeting came at Cane Ridge, Kentucky. The camp meetings are best known for the unusual phenomena reported such as the "jerks," the "barks," and others. Peter Cartwright and other Methodist circuit riders continued to utilize the camp meeting in frontier regions. By 1811 as many as 500 camp meetings were held throughout the frontier.

In addition, during the Second Great Awakening Charles Finney made a profound impact on the Christianity of his and subsequent generations. Finney witnessed many amazing episodes of revival. Finney began many of what were called "new measures," including public altar calls and protracted meetings.

The 1857-58 Awakening is perhaps the least known in the modern era. It is also called the Layman's Prayer Revival because of the union prayer meetings which began in New York City. In the fall of 1857 lay missionary Jeremiah Lanphier passed out handbills inviting others to pray. The first meeting was at noon on September 23 at the North Dutch Reformed Church. Within six months *fifty thousand* gathered in small groups across New York for prayer. Several thousand also met in Philadelphia and other cities. Other features included church revivals in Massachusetts and South Carolina as well as Canada, Presbyterian conferences focussing on revival, and aggressive Sunday School campaigns.

Newspapers reported widely on the revival. The Washington, D.C. *National Intelligence* filed this report: "The Revivals, or Great Awakening, continue to be the leading topic of the day . . . from Texas, in the South, to the extreme of our Western boundaries and our Eastern limits; their influence is felt by every denomination."[18] This revival had a profound impact on the ministry of evangelist D.L. Moody.

Orr said "the Awakening of 1904-08 "was the most extensive Evangelical Awakening of all time."[19] The best known feature of this awakening was the Welsh Revival. The prominent person in the revival was Evan Roberts, a coal miner/ministry student. At a meeting in 1904, Roberts cried out to the Lord "Oh, God bend me." God did bend him and used him throughout Wales. In less than six months over one hundred thousand came to Christ as a result of this movement of God.

At the same time many places in America reported revival. For example, the Texas *Baptist Standard* featured articles concerning revival in Houston, Waco, and Marshall. Evangelists such as R.A. Torrey and J. Wilbur Chapman reported unusually successful crusade efforts. In addition, Pentecostalism was born as well, although opinions about this movement range from those who call it a revival to those who call it a debacle.

The Influence of Revival Accounts

Past accounts of revivals can greatly aid the ministry of the evangelist. They encourage us that God is still at work in history. They remind us that God uses all types of people. They spur us to greater faithfulness and commitment to God.

Jonathan Edwards wrote his *Faithful Narrative* to describe revival in 1734-35. Half the town was converted in one year's time. John Wesley read the *Faithful Narrative* in 1738, soon after it was available in England. Wesley was so moved by it he was led to pray for a similar movement of God to touch England.

Edwards also wrote *A Humble Attempt to Promote Explicit Union in Visible Prayer*. Several decades after its publication Isaac Backus and others read it. As a result they sent out a circular letter signed by a number of New England ministers. Also, Jonathan Goforth, the famous missionary, was compelled to enter the mission field after reading the writings of Charles Finney.

Why Study Revivals of the Past?

There are several reasons for studying past revivals or awakenings:

(1) They teach us the true meaning of revival. Revival is not a series of meetings held at a local church and led by a guest preacher. Revival is the sovereign activity of God bringing His people to repentance and brokenness, resulting in a fresh, powerful ministry in service and evangelism. While God will at times use special services to touch His children in a new way, He is not bound to do so. This reminds us to depend on Him, not on our services, ability, planning, etc., as important as these may be.

(2) They remind us of the kind of people God will use in revival. Someone has said, "God does not have favorites, He has intimates." Studying the diversity of people used by God in mighty revival demonstrates this truth. Read Jonathan Edwards and admire his brilliance, but read the letters of D.L. Moody and admire that God could use a man with such atrocious grammar! Some, like George Whitefield and Shubel Stearns, were spellbinding speakers. Others ranted and raved and caused near bedlam when they preached. These men faced tremendous difficulty for the cause of Christ: poor health, opposition, persecution, demanding schedules, and minimal resources. Once after preaching in London in the face of tremendous opposition, Whitefield wrote, "I was blessed of God to have rocks, stones, and pieces of dead cats thrown at me today."

(3) They remind us of our need of others. One of the most fascinating aspects of the First Great Awakening to me is how the main leaders knew one another and visited whenever possible for support and encouragement. Frelinghuysen in New Jersey is credited with experiencing the first sparks of the awakening's fire in the year 1726. His work encouraged George Whitefield and Gilbert Tennent. Whitefield also had close contact with the Tennents in Pennsylvania and with Edwards in Massachusetts. I have often told my students the little saying, "If you run with dogs, you will get some fleas." Stated positively and less idiomatically, if you spend time with people who have a passion for revival, it will inevitably influence you positively. One discipline I have kept for years is to read a biography annually of a great evangelist or a leader in revival like Edwards. How my heart is stirred by reading about these men of God!

(4) These revivals give us true accounts to tell as we preach. Stories from the great awakenings and other revivals can be powerful in revival services. For example, when preaching on the subject of revival, I have often used the following principles for personal revival shared by Evan Roberts during the Welsh Revival of 1904-05: (a) Confess every known sin; (b) Put away every doubtful habit; (c) Obey the Holy Spirit promptly; and (d) Proclaim the Lord Jesus publicly.

(5) Specific accounts of church revivals or college awakenings from the pen of men like Jonathan Edwards and J. Edwin Orr give stirring testimony to the power of God to change lives. The stories of revival in the past can be used to prepare the church where you will be preaching in the future. The role of prayer in

revival is an example. For example, you can tell about the time Isaac Backus drafted a letter which was circulated to ministers throughout New England in the late 1700s. The letter stated:

> To the ministers and churches of every Christian denomination in the United States, to unite in their endeavors to carry into execution the *humble attempt to promote explicit agreement and visible union of God's people in extraordinary prayer for the revival of religion and the advancement of Christ's kingdom on earth.*
> In execution of this plan, it is proposed that the ministers and churches of every Christian denomination should be invited to maintain public prayer and praise, accompanied with such instruction from God's Word, as might be judged proper, on every first Tuesday, of the four quarters of the year, beginning with the first Tuesday of January, 1795, at two o'clock in the afternoon, if the plan of concert should then be ripe for a beginning, and so continuing from quarter to quarter, and from year to year, until the good Providence of God prospering our endeavors, we shall obtain the blessing for which we pray.[6]

This concert of prayer was followed by many churches, playing an important role in the beginnings of the Second Great Awakening. The italicized section is a direct quote from the title of an earlier treatise by Jonathan Edwards, demonstrating once more the impact the writings on previous revivals can have on the future;

(6) The accounts of past revivals can guide you concerning how to lead when genuine revival does come. Suppose God sent a mighty revival in the next place you preach to the extent that scores of individuals begin confessing sin, scores more were converted, and restitution was made. What then? An awareness of the past can help give insight. That is not to say that God always repeats His activity precisely; but there is certainly a consistency to the Word of God and to prior activity of God in history. Such awareness can help to deepen the revival beyond emotional catharsis to a continuous growing encounter with Christ. Part of the way you can encourage revival when it comes is to tell the account of past movements. Jonathan Edwards said, "Nothing tended more to promote the work of grace among the people at Northampton, than to tell them what God was doing in other places."[21]

(7) More than anything, your study of historic revivals will change *you*. Why not begin now with a commitment to use some

of the time on the road in a revival service, or the time you use to prepare for a meeting, to read about past revivals?

Resources on Revival

If you are convinced, and I hope you are, that studying the past movements of God is an important discipline, let me suggest some possible resources. By no means is this a complete list—these are books with which I am personally familiar and that are either in print or readily found in most theological libraries.

1. Surveys or Overviews of Revivals in History:

Beougher, Timothy K. and Alvin L. Reid. *Evangelism for a Changing World.* Harold Shaw, 1995. While dealing with other subjects, one third of this book surveys modern awakenings.

Cairns, Earle E. *Endless Line of Splendor: Revivals and Their Leaders from the Great Awakening to the Present.* Tyndale, 1986. This book is the best recent overview of awakenings.

Ecklund, Bob. *Spiritual Awakenings.* This little book published by the Home Mission Board (SBC) gives a succinct overview of American awakenings.

Orr, J. Edwin. *Campus Aflame.* International Awakening Press, 1994.

2. Books which analyze or explain revival:

Coleman, Robert E. *The Spark That Ignites.* World Wide Press, 1989.

Roberts, Richard Owen. *Revival!*

Murray, Ian. *Revival and Revivalism.* Banner of Truth, 1994. A Presbyterian analyzes revival from 1750 to the present.

3. Sources on specific awakenings:

First Great Awakening

Edwards, Jonathan. *The Works of Jonathan Edwards.* ed. Spirero Dwight, Banner of Truth, 1987, originally published in 1834, the recent edition is affordable, although the print type is small. This two-volume set includes all the major writings of Edwards. Key titles, many of which can also be purchased separately, include:

—*Faithful Narrative of Surprising Conversions*
—*Some Thoughts on the Present Revival of Religion*
—*An Humble Attempt to Promote Visible Union*

Whitefield, George. *George Whitefield's Journals*. Banner of Truth, 1960

Second Great Awakening:

Finney, Charles G. *Lectures on Revival of Religion*. Many published editions of this are in print.

Prayer Revival of 1857-58:

Orr, J. Edwin. *The Event of the Century: The 1857-58 Awakening*. ed. Richard Owen Roberts, Wheaton: International Awakening Press, 1989.

Revival of 1904-08 (Including the Welsh Revival):

Orr, J. Edwin *The Flaming Tongue: Evangelical Awakenings 1900*. Moody, 1975.

The Twentieth Century:

Avant, John, Malcolm McDow, and Alvin L. Reid, eds. *Experiencing God in Revival: Brownwood, Fort Worth, Wheaton and Beyond*. Nashville: Broadman and Holman, 1996. This is the account of a powerful revival beginning in Brownwood and spreading to colleges and churches across the nation.

Culpepper, C. L. *The Shantung Revival*. The Home Mission Board of the Southern Baptist Convention published a small edition of this account of a powerful revival in China in the 1930s.

4. Biographies

Dallimore, A. *George Whitfield: God's Anointed Servant in the Great Revival of the Eighteenth Century*. Crossway 1990.

Finney, Charles G. *The Autobiography of Charles G. Finney*. Bethany, 1977.

Murray, Ian. *Jonathan Edwards: A New Biography*. Banner of Truth 1991.

Pollock, John. *John Wesley*. Northwind, 1995.

Endnotes

1. See John Avant, Malcolm McDow, and Alvin Reid, eds., *Revival: The Story of the Current Awakening in Brownwood, Fort Worth, Wheaton, and Beyond* (Nashville: Broadman and Holman, 1996), for more about this movement.

2. Norman Grubb, *Rees Howells: Intercessor* (Christian Literature Crusade, 1980).

3. Albert H. Newman, *A Hitory of the Baptist churches in the United States* (Philadelphia: American Baptist Publication Society, 1898), 271.

4. *National Intelligence* (Washington), Zomarch 1858, 1.

5. J. Edwin Orr, *The Flaming Tongue* (Chicago: Moody, 1975), 191.

6. Cited in Arthur B. Strickland, *The Great American Revival* (Cincinnati: Standard Press, 1934), 45.

7. Cited in Martin Moore, *Boston Revivals 1842* (Reprint: Richard Owen Roberts, 1980), vii.

Alvin L. Reid, at the time of this writing, was Assistant Professor in Christianity and occupant of the John R. Bisagno Chair of Evangelism at Houston Baptist University. He is presently Associate Professor of Evangelism and Church Growth and occupant of the Bailey Smith Chair of Evangelism at Southeastern Baptist Theological Seminary in Wake Forrest, North Carolina.

Preparing Sermons Through Bible Study

The call to preach is a call to prepare. This axiom echoes the wisdom found in numerous preaching textbooks as well as the testimonies of some of the greatest preachers in the history of the Church. Sermon preparation requires study. Billy Graham has said in various settings that, if he had his ministry to do all over again, he would study more.[1] We preachers ought to continue to be good students all our lives.

Since we are called to preach the Bible, we ought to study the Bible. This is no mere platitude. It is based on our Christian experience. We learned about Christ through the scriptures and our experience was confirmed by the witness of others who had believed on Him as well.[2]

We speak that which we know, so we speak more effectively from Scripture when we have studied. When I preached my first sermon, I did what many preachers do—I told them everything I knew about the Bible and Christian duty in 12 minutes. Why twelve minutes? I told them twice. Then the truth dawned upon me: I had to preach for the rest of my life and I had told them everything I knew and had nothing else to say. I would have to study and learn more to say in future sermons. Right then I resolved to study. That decision led me to an exciting adventure.

All preachers should resolve early in ministry to study the Bible. Otherwise, you will soon run out of something meaningful to say. Indeed, the study of the Bible ought to be a part of a larger life of study.[3] "Be prepared!" is a good motto for preachers as well as Boy Scouts.

Preachers study the Bible for many reasons: (1) to achieve a general awareness of its contents; (2) to find specific information about certain persons, places, or events in the Bible; (3) to discover more details on favorite subjects; (4) to develop our own acquaintance with the Bible, and (5) for our own spiritual growth. Above all, though, preachers ought to study the Bible because of our call to preach its truth and make application of that truth to the lives of the individual listeners. The nature of this preaching ministry requires a consistent, systematic program of study. Thus the purpose of this chapter is to present a Bible study plan for sermon preparation.

The plan proposed in this chapter employs the grammatical-historical-theological method of hermeneutics. Because sermon preparation requires more than pure exegesis, the schema includes a fourth element, the practical, or homiletical component.

Gather the Resources

A craftsman always begins by acquiring the proper tools for his task. This is a must for the preacher in the preparation of sermons. Begin by selecting a favorite version of the Bible. Use its verses for reference during exegesis. Choose one which you know to be accurate and reliable. In this author's preaching delivery classes at Southwestern Baptist Seminary, the *New International Version* is the translation of choice. Keep the Hebrew and Greek texts nearby and read from them as much as possible. A good lexicon and a grammar will be necessary for reading the originals. Other tools include an English dictionary, a word study book for each testament, a concordance, a Bible dictionary, an encyclopedia, and an atlas of the Bible lands. For the historical background of individual books, have on hand Old and New Testament introductions. Select some commentaries which include introductory sections. Choose a good one-volume commentary for brief background information. Some study Bibles also contain good introductory material.

Commentaries are necessary for the verse-by-verse study. Individual book commentaries from different sets, as a rule, prove to be more useful than those from the same collection. Book commentaries provide more detailed information than one volume on the whole Bible can include. In addition, purchase some books of sermons. They offer the fruit of the study of other preachers. A couple of words of caution are in order here: (1) Resist the temptation to repeat the sermons of well-known preachers; (2) Refer to sermons late in the process of preparation, when your own ideas already are formed and your own creativity will not be stifled by different thoughts on the same passage.

Include a systematic theology and one of each testament in your resources. These texts will give a comprehensive overview of the contents of the Bible and will show how certain doctrines are developed throughout Scripture. They also will offer controlling themes for interpreting the Bible. For example, consider Covenant theology or Kingdom theology.

With reference materials ready, you are ready to begin the journey from text to sermon. Begin in prayer and commit to the Spirit's leadership. He is involved in the process from the start.

Read the Text Carefully

Begin sermon preparation by reading the text twenty or twenty-five times. Read the reference version first, then read others for comparison. Someone suggested thinking of the Bible as a place where you go to visit, to meet your friends, to see the places, to hear the sounds. We may think of this as entering the world of the text. Listen to the people who live there tell their own stories. Stay awhile; linger in the world of the text until you are a part of it and it is a part of you. Then you can return to tell the listeners what life is like there. We often hurry to the formation of the sermon after rushing through the text, distilling the text, and determining the central idea. We ought to determine the major idea in each sermon text, but not too early in the process. We should read for understanding the fullness of meaning of the text in its context instead of merely trying to "boil it down" to one idea. The Bible is more than a series of ideas; it has a story line providing connection and continuity.

At this point in the reading begin noticing the form of the text; it will become a factor in the shape, or structure, of the sermon. We tend to think of preparing the sermon structure only after the completion of exegesis. Such practice may lead to the separation of hermeneutics and homiletics, exegesis and sermon, when the ideal is to progress from text to sermon. The practice of extracting an idea from the text for purposes of discussion prompts us to subdivide and explain the *idea* in the sermon and keeps us from allowing the text to supply or suggest its own pattern of organization.

As you read, experience the text. Try to feel the mood of the scripture. Rejoice with Jesus when people who heard him brought the children to him (Mark 9:33-39). Feel the sharp pain of sorrow that David felt at the report of the death of his son Absalom (2 Samuel 19:1-7). Sense the indignation of Jesus when he drove the money changers from the temple (Mark 11:15-18). Share the frustration of Job when his friends chided him for his sin (Job 6:1-30), or Jonah when he sat outside the recently-converted Nineveh (Jonah 4:1-11). Remember what happens to you as you live inside the text. When writing the sermon, try to recreate through your words that same experience through words for those who will listen to your sermon. At the same time, determine the purpose of the text. What is the text doing? The purpose of a text should become the purpose of the sermon. Good preaching is purposeful preaching.

While reading a text, try to set aside temporarily your own presuppositions about its meaning. Do not attempt to tell the text what it means or what you think or want it to mean. Allow the text to present its own message, its own meaning. It may correct, alter, or invalidate your beliefs, or validate and confirm them. A wise old missionary in a chapel sermon held up the Bible and pointed to it. He said wryly: "This book will shed a lot of light on some of the books on your library shelf." We do not study the Bible to prove ourselves right; we study it to find what is right.

We read in order to understand the text. At some point we need help from others who have read.

Search for Meaning

Upon completion of a thorough reading of the text, write a complete statement of its meaning. Then employ components of the grammatical-historical-theological method to increase your understanding. Begin with a serious linguistic and structural (grammatical) study of the text. Start with words, the basic building blocks of language. Explore definitions, etymology, and usage of words. Determine the relationship of words in a sentence (syntax). In Greek the location of the verb, for example, has much to do with emphasis in a sentence, especially when it comes as the first word.

Study the grouping of words in phrases and clauses of the text. Remember that the punctuation which marks phrases and clauses in various translations was not a part of the languages of the Bible. Study the sentences of the text. Sometimes this is a challenge due to length, as in the opening verses of Ephesians. Identify parts of the sentences. Read them aloud to get a feel for phrasing. The biblical text, after all, was speech placed in print. The printed word may have run-on sentences because that was how people talked.

Discover the units of thought in the text. A lectionary will help identify these blocks. Compare these with the paragraphs of some translations. Consider that paragraph markings and chapter divisions do not always indicate the completion of a unit of thought. Read the first part of Hebrews twelve as a continuation of chapter eleven and think about the meaning of the "great cloud of witnesses."

Diagram the text. An alternative to the complex and difficult grammatical diagram is the structural diagram of the text, with the proper nouns, verbs, and other "heavier" parts of speech aligned with the left margin.[4] This diagramming may be done in the original languages or in English. A diagram is an outline of meaning. Refer to it while reviewing summaries of the teachings of the text in its context written earlier in the study.

The search for meaning also should include the historical and theological components of hermeneutics. Study the text in its context. For its historical, social, and geographical setting, consult an introduction to the testament in which a text is found. Determine the author, nature, purpose, destination, and recipients of the Bible book in which it is located. Refer to dictionaries and encyclopedias for further information. Read the chapters which precede and follow the sermon passage. Discover how the text fits into the continuity of the entire Bible, the book, and the chapter. Conduct a verse-by-verse study of the text. Look to the commentaries for assistance.

Turn to theology texts and summaries in commentaries for interpretative statements and for discussion of the grand themes of the Bible and the development of those themes in specific books. Compare the interpretations offered there with your own, which you wrote after reading the text numerous times and before you turned to other resources for assistance. Watch for confirmation and validation of meaning, but do not refuse correction or alteration of your own views. The collective wisdom of the scholars who have studied the Bible across the centuries will enrich our own study.

The structural diagram, summary of meaning, and definition of the purpose of a text complete the exegesis. To complete the sermon, however, more work is necessary. The practical, or homiletical component is the next vital part of the process.

Design the Sermon

The next step is to design the sermon. Usually this means crafting an outline. Before sketching this outline, revise the summary of the meaning of the text which you wrote during exegesis. Read passages in *The Living Bible*, a paraphrase, or *The "Cotton patch" Gospel* of Clarence Jordan for examples of restating a text in contemporary language. Attempt to state this meaning in one complete sentence—even if it is a long, compound, complex sentence. Make the statement comprehensive; do not omit any part of the text. This sentence is indispensable to the sermon. In fact, it is the sermon in a sentence. Then add a sentence declaring the purpose of the text. Make that purpose the aim of the sermon. Purposeful preaching is stronger preaching. Have a clear aim in each sermon. This aim will lead to a natural call for response at the time of the invitation. The sermon in a sentence has become the central idea of the sermon. It tells what the sermon is about. The sermon, then, is an explanation, illustration, and application of this idea. The purpose statement indicates the desired outcome of the sermon. It indicates what the hearer ought to do, understand, or become as a result of hearing the sermon. The summary sentence and purpose statement direct the final stages of sermon preparation.

Sketch a sermon outline, following the contents and design of the text carefully. A good way to formulate this outline is to revise the structural diagram. Rewrite it, using present-tense language. Use sentences instead of key words in the outline because sentences are complete expressions of thought. They do not have to be long. Indeed, short sentences help achieve clarity in preaching. Key words are good devices for remembering the sermon, for the listener as well as for you. A word alone, however, does not make a good sermon point. The three-point, one-word alliterative outline sermon structure is weaker than the sentence outline for at least two reasons: (1) texts are not structured that way; and (2) people do not comprehend words as well as they understand sentences. Preachers often outline the contents of the text and preach that outline to their people, thus teaching them what the text says. Such outlines tend to be highly explanatory in nature, with the material presented in the past tense. To be sure, teaching the text is important. Scripture content outlines, though, sometimes lack contemporaneity and the appeal which comes with the use of present tense.

Express in writing how you felt during the study of the text. That feeling is the meaning of "experiencing the text." Remember your emotions. Did you want to cry or to laugh? Were confession and repentance the only proper responses? Did you feel empty or did satisfaction fill your soul? Consider, for example, the experience of the woman at the well in the fourth chapter of John, a favorite evangelistic passage. Can you identify with her surprise, her dismay, her amazement, her shock, her belief, her joy, her impulse to tell her story? Can you identify with Jesus' insight into her spiritual condition, his patience, longsuffering, gentleness, firmness, confidence, and sense of identity with the woman's tradition as he talked with her? Can you sense the indignation of the disciples when they returned? Can you feel a twinge of guilt over preoccupation with physical hunger which caused you to miss Jesus' meaning when he spoke of thirst for living water? When we begin to desire that our listeners experience the text with us, we are ready to put the finishing touches on the sermon.

Finish the Sermon

Write the sermon by filling in the details of the design. Relive your encounter with the text. Plan for the sermon to tell how the text will make the same impact on those who hear you preach that it made on you. Preaching is telling the truth of the Scripture to the people who live in a different place in a different time. That act of declaring truth to the listener is the goal of Bible study for sermon preparation.

The preacher is obligated to know about two worlds—the world in which we live and the world of the text.[5] Sermon preparation is incomplete until the preacher expresses the meaning of the text, discovered through study, to the listeners.

So, then, on the basis of the study, write the sermon. The sermon needs a proper beginning (introduction), middle portion (body), and ending (conclusion). With words, sentences, paragraphs, complete the design of the sermon. Strive to achieve clarity, simplicity. The speaking of words which capture the meaning of Scripture, accompanied by the breathing of the Spirit upon our words to make them live brings about an event in which God comes to the people. Explain the text. Illumine its meaning with illustrations from the Bible, history, personal experience, current events, great literature, and, yes, poetry. Make direct statements of application to the individual. Conclude with an invitation, an appeal for decision.

Throughout the entire process remember to pray and rely on the Holy Spirit to enable your understanding. Nothing in this chapter is meant to overrule or ignore the work of the Spirit. Begin in prayer. Allow time in the process for reflection and meditation. The Spirit is our teacher. He is our guide. He works in us as we prepare and we trust him to work in the listeners as we preach.

Endnotes

1. John Stott reports that he heard Graham say this to a gathering of about 600 clergy in London in 1979. See John R. W. Stott, *Between Two Worlds* (Grand Rapids, MI: William B. Eerdmans Publishing Company, 1982), 181.

2. See Paul Scott Wilson, *The Practice of Preaching* (Nashville: Abingdon Press, 1995), 125.

3. See the excellent discussion of this point by Fred B. Craddock in *Preaching* (Nashville: Abingdon Press, 1985), 69-83.

4. For help with "Syntactical and Homiletical Analysis," as well as "Exegetical Outlines," see Walter C. Kaiser, Jr., *Toward an Exegetical Theology* (Grand Rapids, MI: Baker Book House, 1982), 89, 150, 166-81, and Walter L. Liefeld, *New Testament Exposition* (Grand Rapids, MI:

Zondervan Publishing House, 1984), 45-56, 155-66. Their suggestions accomplish what we mean by structural analysis. Following their plans helps make the move from text to sermon with greater ease.

5. See Stott, *Between Two Worlds*, 135-79. Stott's controlling metaphor is that of building a bridge from the world of the text to the contemporary world. The original title of his book, as first published in England, is *I Believe in Preaching*.

James L. Heflin is Professor of Preaching at Soutwestern Baptist Theological Seminary in Fort Worth, Texas.

Preparing Sermons for a Revival Meeting

The answers to the mystery of evangelistic preaching may reside in the mind of God. However, the burden of that preaching grips the hearts and minds of preachers to the point that there is "fire in their bones," and they "can do no other." Indeed, preaching in a revival meeting is more than simply an exercise that a preacher fulfills at the appointed times throughout the revival week. It is not some oratorical relic of the past that was relevant for Paul, Bernard, Luther, Whitefield, Wesley, Finney, and Moody. Evangelistic preaching is God's method of proclaiming the revealed gospel in Jesus Christ to estranged, alienated, and lost members of the human race for the purpose of reconciliation to the Holy God.

As the evangelist approaches the preparation of the revival meeting sermon, he needs to remember that he brings six things to the table; namely, his personal life, sermon preparation, content, organization, delivery, and style.[1]

Preparing the Preacher

The Preacher Is Indispensable. Paul forever stamped this importance upon preaching when he wrote, "How shall they hear without a preacher?"² Because the preacher is an irreducible component in preaching, he must be prepared to bring to the pulpit the elements within his responsibilities. There are no excuses for watered-down, anemic, slipshod, evangelistic sermons. The messenger must remember who he represents as he stands in the pulpit. He also must remember that Jesus is the unseen member of every congregation. The preacher is not to please the people; he is to please Jesus. What does Jesus say about this sermon? Is He pleased with my life as I prepare and deliver the message? Is He pleased with the content? Is He pleased with the way it is delivered? In concise terms, is Jesus pleased? The responses during the time of the invitation, at times, may answer these questions. The preacher gets that for which he preaches. When he preaches for decisions, he ordinarily gets decisions. Everything in the sermon must point to the invitation. Therefore, as the preacher prepares and preaches the message, he must keep the invitation in mind. He does this when he focuses on Jesus Christ for the content and the lost in the congregation as the hearers.

The Preacher Is God's Messenger. The evangelistic sermon is not something to be tasted, enjoyed, and discarded. It is a challenge and an appeal from a messenger who is sharing from the inner recesses of his soul about subjects of eternal consequences to the souls of men and women who have eternal qualities. The sermon is the summation of the preacher's walk with God and his view on the sinfulness of man. In this scenario, the preacher is the voice from God and not an echo of man.

The Preacher Is Marked with Urgency. The effective evangelistic preacher is filled with urgency. Without urgency, there is little impact. Urgency can be illustrated through the math formula $MV=I$.³ The spiritual application is $MU=R$.⁴ Urgency does not necessarily mean volume. Urgency comes from an enslaved heart of the messenger captured by the Holy Spirit and sent on a divine mission of proclamation.

The Preacher Declares Truth. Phillips Brooks said, "Preaching is the Communication of truth by men to men."⁵ He further stated, "It has in it two elements, truth and personality. Neither of those can it spare and still be preaching."⁶ In the sermon, God provides the truth. The preacher provides the personality.

Brooks' definition indicates that the New Testament evangelistic sermon is a living entity or it is not a New Testament evangelistic sermon. To the degree the sermon pulsates with life, to that degree the sermon has life-transforming power. The sermon that lives is the culmination of the divine life of God touching the human life of the chosen communicator who in turn shares that touch, and what that means, with those who are in need of a kindred touch from God.

The Preacher Is Disciplined. How does the preacher achieve these things? There is only one answer - WORK! WORK!! WORK!!! Sermon preparation is like giving birth to a baby - they are both born in labor.

The effective preacher does not approach the sermon with indifferent attitudes and undisciplined habits. He knows that this spiritual work is far too big for him in his own resources. When he starts out preaching, he might wonder why everyone in town does not take advantage of his oratorical skills. After he becomes a seasoned warrior in the pulpit, he wonders why anyone in town would even bother to come to hear him.

Preparation of the Sermon for a Revival Meeting

In general, preparation of the sermon for a revival meeting is the entire journey through life. In particular, it is that exercise in the germination and the development of the idea of a particular message. In fact, the three basic elements of sermon preparation are: germination of the idea, development of the sermon, and preservation of the materials.

Germination of the Idea. The origin of the sermon idea can come from a plethora of sources. It may originate from Scripture, personal experience, observation, congregational need, current event, nature, church calendar, or reading printed material. At times the idea may be the result of an instant spark of inspiration. However, these are few and far between. Ordinarily, the sermon idea is the result of diligent labor. Regardless, without an idea, there is no sermon.

Development of the Idea. When the idea emerges, the preacher must allow the subconscious to work and employ conscious awareness to ponder and expand the idea. The alert messenger writes down related ideas, gathers thoughts from human experiences, and collects relevant anecdotes. In addition, he exegetes the text, reads commentaries, books, newspapers, periodicals, magazines, and listens to people as they talk. One of the best ways to develop an evangelistic sermon is to have a consistent personal witnessing lifestyle. There is no better way to learn human nature than through witnessing. This prepares the preacher with a deeper understanding of the mind, opinions, and rationale of the lost person. Witnessing will revolutionize the preaching of an evangelistic messenger.

Preservation of Materials. It is crucial that the preacher develops an effective method of material preservation. It is true that many good sermon ideas have been lost because they were not written down when they came to mind. The preacher should, if possible, carry a small tape recorder to record any sermon thoughts that might come to mind as he is involved with other matters. In addition, the computer is an excellent filing system. File folders and a good catalog system for the preacher's library will save endless hours of preparation. The messenger should use the method or combination of methods that is best suited for his purposes.

Content of the Revival Meeting Sermon

The content of the revival meeting sermon does not center upon abstract ideas, but upon concrete realities. The heart cry of the person in the pew is the age-old question, "Is there any word from the Lord for me today?" God's messenger can stand in the pulpit with confidence and proclaim, "Yes, God has a word for you. Here it is." When the people ask for bread, the preacher must not offer sand. When the people ask for water, the preacher must not offer dust. When the sermon content shackles the heart of the preacher, it will most assuredly move the heart of the lost person to Jesus Christ. In order to achieve this, the content has no less than five qualities.

Content Must Be Biblical. The content must be built upon the revelation of God which is contained in the Bible. The preacher is not given the license to preach as he pleases. He is called of God to proclaim His divine intention of reconciliation. Human ideas, philosophies, abstractions, and ingenuity may stimulate the mind, but they will never move the human heart to God. Jesus said, "Without Me, you can do nothing."[7] When the sermon content is Biblical, the Holy Spirit uses the message to fulfill His purpose. God promises to bless His word, not man's ideas. The effective evangelistic preacher is not only Biblical in content but also is true to Biblical principles. In the application of the message, the preacher must not say or promise things that are not true to Biblical teachings. Indeed, honesty is the best policy. Jesus never sugar-coated, lowered the standards, or watered down the gospel to attract followers. He offered the challenges that required life surrender.[8]

Content Must Be Clear. The main function of the sermon is to interpret the mind of God to the people. Clarity is indispensable in order to fulfill this function. Clarity depends upon the preacher's understanding of the mind of God and human needs. The clear evangelistic sermon can not be detached from the preacher. He will prepare the message based upon who he is as a person, how he lives, what he thinks, his philosophies of life and ministry, and what he believes. Clarity is the product of his personal experience with God. This element distinguishes the preacher from being an echo of ideas and a voice for God. No preacher can preach beyond his personal experience with God. The sermon becomes hollow and is marked by spiritual inertia. Content of experience filtered through action produces clarity.

Content Must Be Simple. Simplicity does not mean triteness. Simplicity includes understandable language, freshness of thought, energy of style, and relevance of content. The preacher must not be mundane and dull, nor must he be grandiose and pedantic. The congregation should not have to bring a dictionary to the service, nor should it be required to bring alarm clocks. Every renowned evangelist is characterized by the acceptable qualities of simplicity.

Content Must Be Logical. The content of the sermon must stand the test of reason. Faith is the response to intelligent deductions. Every revelation of God to man is logical. The message should be marked by the same quality. The messenger must not make the message so edenic that it is not logical. People live in a real world with real problems and want some real answers. The sermon must focus on reality. The ways by which the preacher is able to accomplish this element is through Biblical content, walk with God, and knowledge of human nature.

Content Must Be Persuasive. The evangelistic sermon must move people to God. This purpose must never be clouded with secondary aims. The sermon is not a demonstration of the preacher's oratorical skill, intellectual capacities, or organizational abilities. The persuasive power of the message rests within the spiritual realm of proclamation. Indeed, the value and persuasion of an evangelistic sermon are lashed to its spiritual purpose. A sermon is never its own excuse for existence. It is to persuade people to turn their hearts home toward God. The preacher achieves persuasion through content, delivery, style, personal walk with

Christ, and personal conviction toward the topic under discussion. If the preacher does not believe it, he will not get the people to believe it. If the evangelist does not practice what he preaches, he will find that it is difficult to get the people to practice it.

Persuasive preaching gets the congregation into the sermon. A persuasive sermon in a revival meeting is a three way participation; namely, God, messenger, and hearers. The statement at athletic events is often made, "The home team has gotten the crowd into the game." The evangelist must get the crowd into the preaching act. Indeed, the pew can ignite the pulpit faster than the pulpit can ignite the pew. However, when the two cooperate to ignite each other, the impact has eternal consequences. This is called persuasion.

Content Must Be Original. The revival sermon must be the product of the mind and heart of the preacher. It is the result of his walk with God, and is the verbal expression of his personal convictions. Originality does not mean preaching ideas that have never been preached before. It means that the message is the product of his labors and not the labors of another. Indeed, the prepared preacher will listen to sermon tapes, read sermon books, study commentaries, scan newspapers, peruse other related materials, but the end product is his. Indeed, the evangelistic sermon is "caught before it is taught."

Organization of the Revival Meeting Sermon

There are six elements that compose the effective organization of a revival meeting sermon: namely, title, text, introduction, body, conclusion, and invitation.[9]

The Title.[10] The purpose of the title is to give direction to the sermon, focus attention on the content, and arouse interest for the message. In an evangelistic meeting, the title is ordinarily not mentioned unless the evangelist does so or it is used in publicity. The title should be relevant to the sermon content, concise in length, attractive in phraseology, and natural in expression.

The Text. From the earliest Christian preaching, scripture has been a vital part, except on occasion during the Middle Ages, of the sermon. One of the most important elements of the sermon is the reading of the text, for the Scripture passage is God's Word to the audience. The sermon is an explanation of the text. The text may be a word, phrase, verse, or extended passage, depending upon the type of sermon. The text is important for content, direction, and sermon organization. It should not be the perennial springboard for the preacher. The text must be the point of development instead of the point of departure. The messenger certainly must not simply wave at the text in passing. Ordinarily, a text of a few verses or extended passage is preferred in a revival message. The longer passage provides a better foundation for the message.

The Text Is God's Word. The gospel of Jesus Christ is the message from God delivered through revelation. The Bible is the written record of that revelation. Consequently, the text is that selected portion of God's Word chosen by the preacher under the inspiration of God's Spirit to serve as the spiritual compass to guide people to the hope, victory, and cure in Christ. The Bible covers, either directly or indirectly, every possible human situation. How God responded to those situations are historical examples of how He can respond to modern situations.

Exegesis and not Eisegesis. The effective evangelistic sermon allows the text to say what it wants to say. Although some eisegesis, which is reading into the text meanings that the text may not communicate, may be acceptable in certain situations, exegesis is the preacher's efforts to determine the truth of the passage, arrange the details in orderly fashion, and communicate that truth.

Allegorizing. This method of determining spiritual meaning for every text has had its times of popularity in Christian history. Again, there are times when this approach might be acceptable; however, it should not be the common practice. The preacher could better use his time discerning the true exegetical meaning of the text than to spend endless hours in mental gymnastics in searching for the spiritual innuendoes of some text. The revival meeting sermon is not an exercise to demonstrate the preacher's ingenuity; it is the declaration of the truth of God. The preacher is to develop the text and not to destroy it.

Familiar Texts. The wise evangelist will use the more familiar texts for the evangelistic sermon. The audience identifies quicker and easier to that with which they are familiar. This does not mean that the preacher should always shun the lesser known Biblical passages, but it does mean that the familiar texts relate quicker to lost people. For example, the passage on the Prodigal Son relates much stronger and faster to a lost person than some Leviticus passage on the Tabernacle.

The Introduction

The introduction must introduce. It must establish the tone for the rest of the revival meeting message. It must be interesting, appealing, arousing, and relatively brief. The introduction can be from one sentence to 10-12 percent of the sermon's content. The length is determined by the sermon and the requirements to introduce the message.

The introduction can start with an illustration, striking sentence, question, description of life situations or explanation of the text. At times, it may be the invitation. The introduction is the first impression the people get of the message. In preaching, first impressions are crucial. A sermon can be developed or devastated by the introduction. Many homilists suggest that the introduction be the last element of the message that the messenger prepares. The rationale is that the preacher has to know what he is going to introduce before he can introduce.

Outline

Importance of The Outline. Outlining is an art. A mediocre sermon can be transformed into an effective message through a good outline. The outline provides order, keeps the preacher from rambling, develops the idea, and provides a means by which the preacher can retain the attention of the audience. Every sermon must have structure, regardless of the number of points. Whether the message has one point or multiple points, the sermon is a disaster without organization and structure.

Announcing the Points. Considerable discussion is offered by homilists in regards to he place of the outline and how to handle the structure as the sermon is preached. On the one hand, some homiletical instructors insist that the outline should be hidden and not announced. On the other hand, some instructors stress that the announcement of a good, well organized, progressive outline is advantageous. The best course is to use the method that is most natural. The effective preacher can use the announcement of the points as attention retainers.

If the preacher decides to announce each point, he should be cautious. If the sermon has, for example, five major points and three sub-points under each major point, announcing each major and minor point would severely distract from the message. In this scenario, only the major points should be announced. The preacher must use wise discretion at this point.

The evangelist needs to remember that many lay people write the sermon title, date, and outline in the margins of their Bibles or on the provided page in the bulletin. A clear, announced outline can greatly strengthen the message, allow the people to follow the message with greater ease, and preserve the sermon material for future spiritual benefit.

Number of Points. The number of points can vary from one to several. The preacher needs to keep in mind that it is easier to prepare a sermon with multiple points and sub-points than with just one point. It is easier to produce material for three main points and two sub-points under each main point than to develop a single idea. In addition, a well organized, multiple point outline is easier to preach. The number of points should be determined by the sermon. Whatever it takes to develop adequately the message should be the number of points.

Alliteration. Some evangelists prefer alliteration. This method of outlining has its advantages. It is an excellent way to keep audience interest. It also helps the preacher to remember the message as he preaches. Some preachers simply have the propensity for alliteration. It is as natural as preaching. For some preachers, the text simply unfolds with ideas that are easily made into an alliterative outline. If the preacher chooses alliteration, he should be cautious not to force the structure. This can be a distraction to the message. It must be natural, progressive, clear, unified, relevant, and accurate to the text and content of the message.

Development of the Outline. The text is the best source to provide the sermon points. As the preacher studies, gathers materials, and starts to prepare the revival message, the outline should be the first thing that he prepares. After the outline is prepared, the preacher should categorize all of the gathered material by marking the material with the appropriate points. As he does the specific preparation of the sermon, he places all of the ideas in logical order under the relevant points of the sermon. Some preachers prefer a written manuscript. Others prefer a detailed outline. The method that is used should be determined by the needs of the preacher. On the one hand, regardless of the chosen method of specific preparation, the evangelist should not read the manuscript. On the other hand, he may want to carry notes to the pulpit with him, depending upon the experience of the evangelist and familiarity with the material.

Application. Every effective evangelistic sermon contains practical application. The wise evangelist does not concentrate upon abstractions, but upon applying God's truths to human situations. These applications may be achieved through appropriate illustrations, addressing contemporary human needs, and answering excuses of lost people. Without application, the sermon loses its appeal. In fact, to the degree the sermon has application to that degree the sermon has impact.

Conclusion

The conclusion is the crescendo, the refrain, the crest of the sermon. Because the conclusion leads into the invitation, the entire message should build to this point. It must be carefully prepared, or it can serve the people broken promises, disappointments, and let downs.

The content can be the summation of the evangelistic sermon, contain stronger application, or a relevant illustration. It must have personal appeal, direct instructions, clarity of thought, and logical progression. It must have the smooth transition into the invitation.

The length of the conclusion depends upon the message. It may be a few sentences or it may be 5 to 7 percent of the message. Whatever it takes to conclude is the barometer to determine the length.

When the preacher uses appeal in the conclusion, he should move from the general to the specific and lesser to the greater in content. Certainly, the preacher should avoid "promises to end" that are broken. The primary purpose of the conclusion is to serve as the valet for the invitation. The preacher must remember that it is far more important for the Holy Spirit to speak to human hearts in the invitation than for the preacher to speak to human ears in the conclusion. In brief, the conclusion is to conclude and not to prolong.

The Style

The style of the revival meeting sermon is as much a part of preparation as the content. Indeed, how the messenger says it is as important as what he says. Good content can be greatly diminished in impact as the result of a poor style. What are the elements of good style? How is a good style developed?

Elements of Style. The preacher must remember that the revival meeting sermon is something to be heard and not read by the audience. Material that is good reading may not be material for good preaching. The sermon builder must remember that the people in the congregation are spending thirty to forty minutes of their lives to listen to what he has to say, and what he has to say should be worth the lives that are spent to hear it. This greatly impacts the preacher's entire approach to preaching.

The style of the sermon is vital to an effective message. It may be narrative, oratorical, literary, or home spun. Regardless, it must communicate. Whereas delivery relates to voice, style relates to the composition of the message.

Communicative. The style must be understandable. People of all ages are in the congregation. It must relate to children as well as adults. One of the greatest compliments that can be paid to the preacher is for a child to say, "I like your preaching." The child may not be able to explain why he or she likes the preaching; however, the child is saying that the preaching communicates. Several questions need to be asked and answered in order to evaluate the clarity of the style. Can a child understand what I am saying? Many of the evangelistic results in a revival meeting will be the decisions made by children. Can a lost person who has never heard the gospel understand the message? Will the medical doctor or college professor listen? Do the people need dictionaries to understand? Will the ushers have to provide pillows? These are just a few questions that need to be addressed. When the message is Biblical, relevant, applicable to life, and interesting, the preacher will more likely succeed in effective communication.

Selection of Words. The preacher must be skillful in the use of words. However, the words are vehicles to deliver the message and not exercises to demonstrate the preacher's ingenuity. The preacher is not a public speaker to entertain audiences, build a personal reputation, and demonstrate oratorical skills. He uses words to call people to God. God deserves and demands our best even in the use of the words we select to communicate the gospel.

A preacher's effectiveness is based, in part, upon the words he uses. This does not mean verbosity. Verbosity does not mean effectiveness. Avoid repetition unless it is used for effectiveness. Say it with as few words as possible. The selection of words comes from the heart, mind, character, purpose of preaching, and walk with God. The messenger uses these elements to mold a message from the heart of God to the hearts of people in order to turn those hearts toward their Holy God and their heavenly home.

The evangelist is not a fax machine of human ideas; he is the messenger of God to transmit God's ideas. In order to do this, he must use strong, vigorous, action-oriented language. Indeed, language is his indispensable equipment. Words become God's spiritual sound waves that strike the hearts of people. They are God's "ignition devices" to jump start a dead soul. Words can arouse emotions and stimulate minds. The sermon is simply words on airwaves to transport people to God. History has been repeatedly changed through the spoken word. The spoken word has challenged men to defy seemingly insurmountable odds, unshackle oppression, and undertake the noblest of causes. When the evangelistic preacher proclaims God's message, his weapons are words anointed with the Holy Spirit. Indeed, "How shall they hear without a preacher?"[11]

Contemporary. The style must be otic or aural. In other words, it is a spoken communication understood by the audience. The use of metaphors, words of action, syllogisms, and contrasting statements are among some ways by which the preacher develops an effective style. The style should be pleasing, informal, natural, exalting, appealing, emotional, and direct.

Developing an Effective Style. The evangelist can use a number of ways to develop an effective style. The study of the masters can provide guidelines for this purpose. However, the messenger needs to understand that style is dynamic; it is in constant transition. The style of Jonathan Edwards was effective in the 18th century, but it is not effective for today. The pictorial styles of Frederick Speakman and F. W. Boreham, or the literary styles of Harry Fosdick or James Stewart, may not be as effective today as they were in the times of the ministries of those men. However, the study of these styles can provide principles that can be applied to the contemporary preacher.

The preacher not only should study the styles of previous generations of preachers but also should listen to the tapes and read the sermons of the current effective evangelistic preachers. The preacher must not emulate these preachers but discern the qualities of word selection. What makes those preachers effective? How do they express their thoughts? What makes them relevant? Why do people listen to them? These are just a few of the questions the preacher can ask as he studies the styles of effective, contemporary preachers.

As the evangelist engages in exercises to build word power, he will reap satisfying benefits. Since words are his weapons, he must constantly improve his arsenal. The primary way by which this is done is study and PRACTICE! PRACTICE!! PRACTICE!!! Practice allows the preacher to shun the pedantic, stilted, grandiose style that detracts. The effective evangelist knows that he is not engaged in exercises of phraseologies, but is involved in preaching the gospel.

In preparing the revival meeting sermon, the effective evangelist knows that if he takes care of the depth of his preaching, God will take care of the breadth of it! God does not build a Paul, John Chrysostom, John Wesley, George Whitefield, D. L. Moody, or Billy Graham on a shallow foundation. Preparation is the preacher's contribution to the cooperative efforts with God to transmit God's message to needy people. Without diligent preparation, the evangelistic sermon is relegated to mediocrity and the results will demonstrate it.

Endnotes

1. Delivery is covered in another chapter.

2. Romans 10:14.

3. Mass times Velocity=Impact.

4. Message times Urgency=Receptivity.

5. Phillips Brooks, *Eight Lectures on Preaching*. SPCK, London, 1959. p.5.

6. Ibid.

7. John 15:5.

8. Luke 9:23.

9. The invitation is discussed in another chapter of this book.

10. For the sake of brevity, the areas of subject and thesis are not discussed in this chapter.

11. Romans 10:14.

Malcolm McDow is Professor of Evangelism at Southwestern Baptist Theological Seminary in Fort Worth, Texas.

Preparing Sermon Illustrations for a Revival Meeting

"Almost all great preaching is characterized by the effective use of illustration. The man who wishes to preach well will cultivate the art of illustrating his sermons."[1]

Revival meeting sermons are like magnificent paintings. With each stroke the painter consults the shaping imagery, plans the method for applying the paint, and then ventures the risk of disrupting all thus far accomplished due to the necessity of another stroke. Multiple factors must be considered. Will this stroke properly contribute to the intended idea of the masterpiece? Is the color the right shade for blending with the scheme? Can this touch of the brush generate the desired impact upon the recipient of the images? Is the canvas prepared and positioned to receive the paint's texture so that the master's imagery is fixed permanently within the material of the canvas? Sound difficult? It is. Do not be disheartened. Few revival Rembrandts are painted on their first canvas.

A sermon for a revival meeting representing God's message to his people in daily living is usually the product of extensive preparation on the preacher's part under the leadership of God's Spirit. A significant effort in preparing revival meeting sermons is locating, shaping, and integrating illustrations into the message. Effective use of illustrations along with the explanation and application of a text gives a sermon that "just right" sound, look, feel. The sermon's satisfaction point is similar to the painter's "Viola."[2] Illustrations are a key aspect of ascertaining the sermon painter's "Viola!" Good illustrations supply a sermon with a sense of satisfaction that allows the preacher to stop the word flow before reaching that point of one too many strokes.

Acting as an illustrator, the preacher obligates himself to bring light on the Scripture text through word windows, assisting those who have eyes to see and ears to hear to know what God is saying to his people. The purpose of this chapter is to guide you to perceive the potential landscape on which the preacher can integrate the art of illustrating into evangelistic messages. The author desires that preachers learn how to find various kinds of illustrations, shape illustrations to match specific ideas in a text, and then import illustrations into revival meeting sermons so that the preacher experiences "Viola!" The people experience "Voila!" God and human beings encounter each other.

What Are We Looking For?

As we embark on a journey toward the purpose and intended desire of this chapter, we would do well to come to a mutual understanding about the meaning of the term illustration. Robert Hastings describes the basic etymology of the verb "to illustrate" as literally meaning "to light up."[3] Michael Hostetler expands this etymology within the context of preaching by defining illustration as "making a verbal foray from the realm of the abstract to the realm of the particular *(or concrete)*."[4] He goes on to say that "illustrating is speaking words in a sermon which substantiate, amplify, explain, or add emotional proof to the points of a sermon."[5]

In the process of defining illustration we unveil insight into the purposes and uses of illustrations. Beyond Hostetler's base list of purposes, illustrations serve to:

> arrest attention, awaken interest, enlist the memory, stimulate imagination, make a definite impression, translate a divine truth into human experience and life, bring the unseen and eternal within the range of ordinary minds, express spiritual things in the language of the senses

and the soul, add to the growing effect of argument, make the truth clearer to listeners so they can apply it to their lives, serve other functional elements, cloth eternal truths in earthly images, provide rest to the congregation in the listening cycle, save time in relating ideas, establish rapport with the people, make repetition possible without weariness, provide a form of reasoning which is clearer to illogical minds, arouse feelings, catch the ear of the utterly careless, facilitate experiential discovery, help the message appeal to all classes of hearers, cause decision making, develop the theme.[6]

To accommodate the above functions illustrations assume a variety of types and sizes. In his discussion on kinds of illustrations, W. E. Sangster says they may take the form of analogy, allegory, fable, parable, historical allusion, biographical incident, personal experience, anecdotes, or figures of speech like metaphor and simile.[7] An illustration's context and function determine its type and the type determines the size. The size may vary from a single word to short phrases, to strings of sentences forming a simple story, or to a few brief paragraphs that communicate the point of the illustration. The size of the illustration can even become as large as life if the preacher chooses to use drama, props, or other visual aids to support the meaning he is trying to relay.

No matter what the function, kind, or size, an illustration must meet certain criteria in order to perform as that "just right" illustration in any given sermon. An illustration must be clear, interesting, accurate, believable, tactful, brief, relevant, fresh, have appropriate emotional appeal, and ability to assist in the interpretation of basic truths.[8]

Now that we know what we are looking for, it becomes important to know how and where to look. Where are you going to find the illustration that has the correct function, shape, and size to suit that major abstract theological idea you seek to undergird? How are you going to find that perfect depicting image that has the right color, the right texture, the right dimensions?

Getting There From Here!

As important as it is to know where to locate illustrations, it is equally important to know how and when one can best transport oneself to the collection points. Criteria for making the best illustrative choices should also be in hand. Simple habits can help you make the "how" portion of illustration collecting relatively easy. The key is to start looking for illustrations ahead of time, preferably two or three months ahead, instead of two or three days before you must preach. Starting early relieves the pressure of having to find the right illustration and having to find it now. This habit also allows the preacher to become acquainted intimately with the illustration insuring that it truly fits the point he is trying to make. Hostetler recommends that the preacher consistently read, study, pray, think, and observe all matters of life in order to support an advanced preparation system.[9]

In the midst of collecting endeavors, the preacher should always be prepared to stop and immediately record an illustrative insight. Carry a note pad or small tape recorder as recording devices. Cut out articles or clippings from paper products that are expendable. For more permanent sources like personal books, write in the margins and on the front or back flaps to record potential illustrative material. L. R. Jenkins suggests that you train the eyes and ears *(all senses)* to observe all situations where an illustrative spark might avail itself.[10]

Coupled with open eyes and ears you need to have an active imagination, a retentive memory, skill in adaption, and a wise restraint.[11] Collecting materials as a result of these practices will create volumes of illustrative gems for implementation at the right moment. Be sure to develop a simple and accessible filing system for your treasure chest of sermon developers.

Where Do We Find That One?

Now you have the "what, how, and when" of illustration collecting. Let us discuss where you look for the treasures to fill your illustration chest. The "where" of it all is a most interesting enterprise. Sangster says there are "no sources of sermon illustration."[12] Through this he infers there is no one place to find that perfect illustration everytime. Instead, Sangster insists that illustrations are everywhere and anywhere. In fact, the chair that you are sitting in right now could act as an illustration of this precise point. So if illustrations are anywhere and everywhere, where do you begin to look for that particular one you need to complete the word pictures required for your sermon?

There are three arenas where illustrations exist. These arenas are: (1) personal experience or close experience with others;

(2) reading, listening to, or looking at the recorded experiences of others; and (3) imagination.[13] These three categories can be divided into source subgroups as follows:

personal experience or close experience with others—walking, traveling, observations from routine activities, nature, pastoral encounters, trying to teach children;

imagination—create your own illustration for the occasion, make it up;

reading, listening, and looking—Bible, newspaper, magazines, poetry, books of literature and short stories, books on history or science or biographies, medicine, fiction, object lessons, printed sermons, epitaphs, taped sermons, hearing great preachers, music, museums, art galleries, drama, movies, bill boards, collections of illustrations on computer, books of illustrations, and the list goes on . . .[14]

Certain precautions apply to the use of each category. For instance, be careful not to use personal experiences to the degree that the attention in your sermon moves from the text to you. When you share from pastoral encounters, never betray a confidence. This will hinder your personal ministry and your preaching.

Be honest about using the experiences of others or your own imagination. Draw upon simple phrases like "a person told me once," "imagine with me for a moment," or "consider the possibility." The preacher should not risk a positive perception of his integrity for the sake of gaining credit for someone else's ideas or by presenting something as actual occurrence that is only hypothetical.

A final precaution regarding the use of illustration collections needs to be stated here. They should not become a crutch. Press your imagination and extend your circle of exposure before running to someone else's pile of treasure. The illustrations extracted from such collections are often stale because they belong to a distant time and place, have generic tones, and lack the luster of personal discovery for the preacher. Nevertheless, when you find life in these sources, use them. They certainly can stir your own imagination. Collected materials also spark interest among church goers if the source of the illustration is connected to a popular figure like R. G. Lee, R. A. Torrey, or Herschell Hobbs.[15] If you consult illustration collections, it is best to find those with crossover indexes that include passages, names, topics, chronological ordering, seasonal occurrences, and contributors. Keeping these precautions in mind, the preacher should make full use of each source category as time permits.

Haddon Robinson associates levels of impact with the major categories of illustration sources.[16] He relates that illustrations of personal experience or close experience are the most powerful. John Broadus speculates that the use of close life-narratives as illustration may be what strengthens the preaching of great revival preachers.[17] This includes preachers like George Whitefield and Dwight L. Moody.[18]

The next level of illustrative power comes from those illustrations closely related to the experience of the listener. Ian MacPherson warns his readers to know what they are talking about when they venture into this domain, less the power be forfeited by inaccurate representation.[19] In other words, do not misrepresent an imagery of plowing to a farmer.

Stepping down another degree, we find that there is power in relating to the listeners from material both they and the preacher have read, heard, or seen. Illustrations from the local newspaper, classic books, or popular movies serve this level well. The least powerful level of impact are those illustrations coming from impressions that only the preacher is familiar with and to which the congregation has little or no exposure.

A deduction from this discussion of illustration sources and their powers of impact is that the experience of the preacher and the people becomes a critical point for powerfully linking the illustration to the text and the text to the lives of the sermon recipients. Therefore, the preacher must leave his castle of books in order to go out into the world of the people. He must leave the world of the people in order to return to the castle, all-the-while relating to God so that God can equip him to use images from the world and the castle to convey the gospel message.[20]

The preacher's life experiences will be limited; his amount of reading, listening, and looking is limited. Yet, he must appeal to a large mixture of personalities and experiences in the lives of the congregants. The preacher leaps this barrier or pins such an adversarial circumstance by injecting a variety of illustrative content into his sermon menu. Though the content, function, type, and size of an illustration will vary, the shape stays relatively the same.

How Do We Shape Illustrations?

Illustrations, like diamonds, are found in the rough. They need delicate cutting. Wayne McDill suggests that the best pattern for selecting illustrations from your treasury first involves a return to the theme you want to illustrate. He says to make sure the theme or point is clearly stated, generalize the concept, brainstorm analogies, and then particularize the illustrative material you select to represent the thought. This process allows the illustrative link to form naturally with the text as it grows out of the subject.

Once the preacher identifies the link, he can then begin to chip away all matter that does not contribute to a brilliant shining upon the intended truth. Exclude extraneous details. Magnify pertinent details. A perfect fit, a match, begins to develop. Bryan Chapell divulges that the most effective features of properly shaped illustrations are: (1) concreteness, (2) movement, (3) creating crisis, (4) concluding, and finally (5) focusing the image on the idea. Adapt the contours of the illustration to accommodate these features.[21]

MacPherson describes the outline of these features as a wedge.[22] However, his imagery is incomplete. The best illustrations take the shape of a diamond. Well-formed illustrations begin at the explained point and end by refocusing on that point for further explanation or application. The middle of the illustration should be the broadest point of illumination that saturates the soul of the listener with the truth being expounded. Whether you want the saturation to move quickly like water off a duck's back or you want it deeply absorbed like a steak marinating overnight in a fine sauce, using words judiciously will create illumination. Describe concretely. Be sensate, specific. Simple, picturesque, modern, and corresponding words are the illustration shapers best tools for cutting his diamonds.[23]

How Do We Integrate Illustrations?

We can find illustrations; we know how to shape them. Now we must consider interweaving illustrations into the flow of the sermon. First, do not dull the gleam of your diamonds with trite introductory statements. Use silence as a transition or simply begin illustrating. The listeners will follow the crisp crackle of good illustrating.

Questions that typically surface concerning integrating illustrations are: (1) "How many should I use?," and (2) "Where is illustration appropriate?" If you think you will receive a blank stare when you make a point, illustrate it. Illustrate meaning in the sermon's introduction, body, or conclusion. Depending on the composure of the congregation, you may want to broadcast a collection of small diamonds that appeal to a cross-section of personalities, or you may choose to project only one choice jewel that unifies the thinking of a major portion of the listening group.

A good rule of thumb that addresses the "when and where" of illustrating is that you illustrate whenever and wherever it is necessary. Two factors influence such necessity: (1) the degree of abstract thought related to a truth; and (2) the mental, emotional, and spiritual complexion of the listeners.

The preacher can usually resolve issues relating to the abstractness of a text with his general knowledge of human nature. Ask yourself, "Does this truth involve simple, compound, or complex ideas?", "Is the point or truth obvious?" Illustrate difficult ideas so clearly even a child can understand.

Insure that your illustrations are clear. Using an illustration that needs further illustration will complicate matters. The way you make an illustration clear is by "taking it into your mind and keeping it there until it is warmed by the heart. Let the illustration live within you until you can feel, breathe, and live every word and action in it."[24] The concern for clarity should exceed the love of a father I know. Each night as he puts his children to bed, he clears the room of any obstructions that might hinder his attempts or the efforts of the children to secure safety during the night in case of a crisis. Integrating clear and pointed illustrations into sermons will clear the path for God's children to perceive his righteousness and mercy.

Considering the second necessity factor is where the revival preacher receives a great challenge. How can one integrate into his sermons illustrative material familiar to a group of people he does not know? Modern technology extends new flexibility to the preacher in getting to know people in another place. For example, you can watch television and learn a great deal about what is happening around and to people in different parts of the world. You can also call the pastor or leaders of the congregation to inquire about the people living in the church community.

Ask about living conditions, occupations, ages, education levels, income, hobbies, common vacation sites for the people, and specific faith interests within the congregation. Ask who cleans the church, mows the lawn, takes care of the nursery. Ask who these people tend to admire and what their affiliation is with local events like sports, rattlesnake roundups, etc. . . . Check the encyclopedia for general information about the closest city or state.

Check maps to see if there are historical or natural monuments in the vicinity. All these indicators help generate an impression of your listeners and can guide you in integrating informed illustrations into your sermons. People notice these efforts and a rapport with hearers quickly develops.

Be careful of assuming that your impression of the preaching context is a perfect copy or exact snapshot of the congregation. Be prepared to adjust your impression of the hearers as you learn to relate to them more effectively. One way Calvin Miller prepares himself for adjustment occasions is by taking an additional list of familiar illustrations along with him to his preaching engagements.[25] He also keeps selected illustrations on the inside covers of his Bible that integrate well into sermons that speak to people where they are.

Henry Ward Beecher is noted for being able to make illustrative adjustments just prior to delivery or even in the midst of preaching.[26] He would watch for the different classes of people. With experienced diagnostic abilities, he would decide if points and illustrations were communicating the meaning and if not, he would shift gears.[27] Beecher could move to another thought location and attempt again to link the listener to the deep things of God. Please don't try this at home—or away from home, unless you are comfortable with discerning group dynamics and can resist the temptation of chasing rabbits. Besides, we cannot all be Henry Beechers!

A more advanced concern in integrating illustrations into revival meeting sermons has to do with the configuration of illustrations as they influence the momentum of single sermons and the overall momentum of a multi-service revival meeting. A helpful idea along this stream of thought is to make early use of a few illustrations from the most powerful illustration category. If you do not gain the listener's attention early and establish rapport quickly in a revival setting, you risk losing the hearer for the rest of the day or week. In the middle of the process you can pace yourself, venture less powerful illustrations with the hope that the tide of previous explanation, illustration, and application will carry the listener toward the climax of the sermon. At the climax, either stack a group of less powerful illustrations together like a bundle of dynamite or come on line with that gripping jewel that drives the specific point of the sermon deep into the life of the pew patrons. Similar momentum serves well for a full week of revival preaching. If you do not start strong, stay strong, and finish strong, chances are life will be the same in that church shortly after you leave. And above all else, remember that God is the redeeming agent through Christ Jesus our Lord and his Spirit should ultimately guide every aspect of what you do when preparing sermon illustrations for a revival meeting.

What Must We Avoid?

Follow the instructions assimilated for you here from a host of preaching practitioners and you will miss a multitude of illustrating potholes. Published lists exist of practices to avoid while illustrating and you need to be aware of their content. However, you will do this compilation for yourself. Seeking out these illustration avoidances on your own will ingrain them more strongly in your thinking and will give you additional exposure to the major works on illustrating key ideas in your sermons. For the sake of time I will assist you by pointing the way to the majority of lists; see: (1) John Edwards' list in *The Art of Illustration Illustrated* (231-33); (2) W. E. Sangster's list in *The Craft of Sermon Illustration* (101-118); (3) Ian MacPherson's list in *The Art of Illustrating Sermons* (164-82); and (4) Bryan Chapell's list in *Using Illustrations to Preach with Power* (148-77).

In The Light Of Others

Before we close the chapter on preparing revival sermon illustrations, you need to know about a tension between homiletical camps in which one group questions if the preacher should even make concerted designs for illustrating. Martin Lloyd-Jones, Henry G. Davis, and Karl Barth resist the practice of illustrating ideas in a sermon. Barth wrote, "Especially unhelpful is the method of seasoning a sermon with all kinds of illustrations. In no circumstance should we hunt around for these!"[28] Their resistance centers around concerns for insulting the intelligence of adult listeners, time, and a fear that the message will suffer or be weakened by illustrations.

Conversely, preachers with the notoriety of Charles H. Spurgeon, Henry W. Beecher, George Whitefield, and Dwight L. Moody strongly support the practice of illustrating sermon material. By example these men lead us to illustrate. Spurgeon claims that the ability to see illustrations is "one of the most important qualifications to be an efficient preacher of the gospel of Christ."[29]

He challenges us to pursue this ability with all our might. Broadus credits "a leading American Preacher" (Beecher) as saying, "he who would hold the ear of the people, must either tell stories, or paint pictures."[30] An illustrating ability helps communicate God's truths well and retentively to those who need to hear the message. Need further evidence? Ask a listener what they remember about the last sermon you preached or they heard.

Thus the homiletical tendencies divide on illustrating. Al Fasol calls for a synthesis, a balancing between the extremes of overuse and no use of illustrations.[31] His words should be heeded as you make your decisions about "how, when, where, and if" you will illustrate.

Practice, Practice, Practice!

Practical exercises that will reinforce advances in illustrating sermons are: (1) listen to good illustrators (not preachers only); (2) study the best illustrations to discover what makes them work; and (3) practice illustrating—read illustrations aloud, write them out and compare them to the source, tell and retell a variety of illustrations again and again in settings other than the pulpit.[32]

The Illustrative Challenge

Choose you this day the manner in which you will serve God as he speaks to the churches. Concede the directing of your words to God's Spirit and you will find yourself in the company of the "Master Illustrator," Jesus himself. Read his parables and notice his use of metaphor in the New Testament.

If you choose not to illustrate, then you will need to look elsewhere for further instruction on how to make the message clear and understandable. If you choose to illustrate, digest the content of this chapter. Then go unto all the world turning on light switches in people's souls, focusing a spotlight on God's truths, and turning a magnifying glass to such an angle that the intensity of light on God's Word starts revival fires burning in the lives of his people.

Endnotes

1. H. C. Brown, Jr., H. Gordon Clinard, and Jesse J. Northcutt, *Steps to the Sermon: A Plan for Sermon Preparation* (Nashville: Broadman Press, 1963), 79.

2. "Viola" is a French word that literally means — There it is! Look! See! Used as an interjection, "Viola" expresses completeness, success, or satisfaction.

3. Robert Hastings, "Use of Illustrations in Preaching, Teaching, and Writing," cassette TC 21C. 1, Nashville: Broadman, 1970.

4. Michael Hostetler, *Illustrating the Sermon* (Grand Rapids: Zondervan Publishing House, 1989), 12. Italics added.

5. Ibid., 16.

6. This list is compiled from multiple sources of homiletical publications discussing illustrations.

7. W. E. Sangster, *The Craft of Sermon Illustration: A Source Book for Ministers* (Philadelphia: Westminster Press, 1950), 27-45.

8. This list is compiled from multiple sources of homiletical publications discussing illustrations.

9. Hostetler, 82.

10. L. R. Jenkins, *450 Stories from Life: A Book of Illustrations* (Philadelphia: Judson Press, 1947), 12. Italics added.

11. John Edwards, *The Art of Illustration Illustrated* (London: Robert Culley, 1909?), 234.

12. Sangster, 53.

13. Hostetler, 47. Also see Ian McPherson, *The Art of Illustrating Sermons* (New York: Abingdon Press, 1964), 122.

14. This list was collected from multiple homiletical publications and then sorted into these categories.

15. Other popular homiletical personalities with published illustration collections are Henry W. Beecher, Craig B. Larson, Halford Luccock, Alexander MacLaren, and Aquilla Webb.

16. Haddon Robinson, *Illustrations: Part One*, cassette TC 13719, *Christianity Today* and *Leadership*, 1988.

17. John Broadus, *On the Preparation and Delivery of Sermons: Fourth Edition*, revised 1979 by Vernon L. Stanfield (San Francisco: Haper & Row, Publishers, 1979), 188.

18. Look at samples of Whitefield and Moody's illustrations provided by Charles H. Spurgeon, *The Art of Illustration* (New York: Wilbur B. Ketcham, 1894), 52-55.

19. Ian MacPherson, *The Art of Illustrating Sermons* (New York: Abingdon Press, 1964), 170.

20. Ian Dixon writes, "The preacher or pastor who hasn't in some sense shared in that world cannot possibly minister to it." In "The Use of Modern Fiction in Preaching and Pastoral Care: Part One," *The Expository Times* 85 (June 1974): 280.

21. See also Al Fasol's section on "General Principles for the Uses of Illustrations in Preaching" in his article titled, "Illustration In Preaching," *Southwestern Journal of Theology* 27 (Spring 1985): 30-31. He offers additional insight for shaping the features of illustrations.

22. MacPherson, 138.

23. MacPherson, 129-33.

24. Jenkins, 12-13.

25. Calvin Miller, *The Empowered Communicator: Seven Keys to Unlocking an Audience* (Nashville: Broadman & Holman Publishers, 1994), 199-200.

26. Broadus (revised 1979), 182. For a contemporary example of adjusting see Gordon MacDonald, "The Day I Brought a Skunk to Church," *Leadership* 4 (Spring 1983): 28-29.

27. MacPherson, 190.

28. Karl Barth, *Homiletics*, trans. Geoffrey W. Bromiley and Donald E. Daniels (Louisville: Westminster/John Knox Press, 1991), 117.

29. Spurgeon, 136.

30. John Broadus, *On the Preparation and Delivery of Sermons*, revised 1898 by Edwin Charles Dargan (New York: A. C. Armstrong and Son, 1903), 160.

31. Al Fasol, 27.

32. MacPherson, 128-36.

Endel Lee is a Ph.D. student in Preaching at Southwestern Baptist Theological Seminary in Fort Worth, Texas and Pastor of First Baptist Church in Roanoke, Texas.

Preparing to Communicate the Message in a Revival Meeting

Preparing to communicate the message in a revival meeting is the last exciting step in an exciting process. The message, strong in its biblical authority, clear and appealing in its style, now must be communicated. The preacher must take three particular phases of communication seriously if the delivery of the message is to be effective. These three areas are: how the message is received, how the message can be received positively, and how the message can be stated clearly.

How the Message is Received

Congregations have three different kinds of listeners. Some people are auditory, some are visual, and some are kinesthetic.

The auditory persons love information. They love to hear biblical word studies, historical background, and doctrinal statements. The explanation of the text is what they like best. They love to learn new things about the Bible. Most auditory persons sit toward the back of the sanctuary. They want as much distance and as little emotional involvement with the preacher as possible during the sermon. This helps them concentrate on the information they receive from the sermon.

The visual person loves illustrations. Whether they be figures of speech or anecdotes, the visual person wants to be able to 'see' what the preacher says. For the visual, analogies and adjectives are important. When limited to explanation of the text only, the visual will say to the preacher, "I just don't *see* what you are trying to say." The visual likes to sit toward the center and to either side of the congregation. Perhaps, this gives the visual a better view of the congregation and of the preacher.

The kinesthetic listeners love emotional involvement. The kinesthetic are the 'amen faces,' the huggers, the backslappers, the optimists. They love to sit front and center where they can see and 'feel' the sermon. They want to relate emotionally to the preacher. For these reasons, the kinesthetic prefers the application portions of the sermon. They want to be told what to do, how to do it, and when to do it.

The kinesthetic also loves the so-called sensory verbs. Sensory words refer to the five body senses: see, hear, smell, feel and taste. In the application portion of the sermon, the kinesthetic responds primarily to phrases such as: "Feel the presence of God," "See the bloodied hands of Christ as He died for you," "Taste the goodness of God," "Hear the Lord crying out".

This description of a congregation is, by necessity, oversimplified. Actually, all three segments of the congregation need and like explanation, illustration, and application. They are distinctive, however, in their preferences. Too many illustrations offend the auditory, too much application offends the auditory and the visual. To communicate the evangelistic message effectively, the preacher will try to balance all three of the functional elements of preaching in every sermon.

To illustrate, I once began an evangelistic sermon by appealing to each segment of the congregation within the first paragraph. I said:

> Not long ago, my college roommate came by my office on a surprise visit and said, "Tell me what you mean by sin and what you mean by the cross," [informational appeal to the auditory]. There he stood, six feet two inches tall, slender, militarily erect, a colonel in the Air Force, and with a somber expression on his face [adjectives to appeal to the visual]. I jumped from my chair, ran to Tom,

hugged him and said, "Tom, you scamp, come in here and sit down" [emotional appeal for the kinesthetic].

I could see each segment of my congregation already deeply involved in the message. A little attention to appealing to all three segments pays dividends in congregational attention.

How to Make the Message Appealing

Most people find difficulty in listening to a monologue, and most preaching is done by monologue. We need to help the congregation all we can. The more appealing the message is, the more likely a positive response will be made to it. Communications experts have long ago identified some factors that help or hinder the appeal of a spoken message.

Predictability, for instance, hinders a positive response to a message. Predictability can occur both in content and in delivery of the sermon. With regard to content, the preacher may have some distracting vocal habits such as periodic clearing of the throat, vocalizing pauses by saying "uh" or "and uh," by using empty words such as "you know." Or the preacher may voice some personal and particular concerns too often. No matter what the text, the occasion, the preacher will find a place to mention one particular issue. When the congregation finds that predictable, the response to the message will be diminished.

Distance is another problem. Distance may occur when preachers speak of things that are not relevant to the congregation. Most congregations, for instance, do not care what life in Israel would have been like if Josiah had not gone out to do battle with the Pharaoh. Or, as Fosdick so ably noted long ago, people don't care what happened to the Jebusites. Distance can also take the form of speaking over the heads of the congregations. Technical theological vocabulary makes people feel the Bible and theology have no bearing on their lives.

When I shared with a friend, years ago, that I had become a Christian, he responded, "So now you are ready for the coming eschaton." I truly could not tell him if I were or were not. The word was new to me and too far removed from my everyday experience for me to care one way or the other.

Communications experts advise us to find 'frames of reference' without congregations. Jesus did this. He referred to a sower, to a steward, to a servant, he described himself as light, truth, the vine and he described Christians as salt and light. Each of his listeners could identify with each of these frames of reference. The frame of reference serves to tell the congregation the preacher is familiar with the world in which the congregation lives and works day by day. The result is, the preacher and the sermon are much more likely to be accepted in a favorable manner.

Source credibility is important to a congregation. That is, can the congregation believe in the preacher? Source credibility involves, among other things, integrity and expertise. The congregation must decide that the preacher will not intentionally mislead them (integrity) and the preacher is biblically sound (expertise). After all, who would want to respond to someone who cannot be trusted or believed?

How to State the Message Effectively

Sermon delivery must always be supportive of content. The use of the voice and the use of body language must be consistent with and supportive of what is being said by the preacher. The relationship between content and delivery is vital. If delivery calls attention to itself, then the preacher has taken precedence over the message. The highest compliment any listener could pay to a preacher is to remember the message and hardly notice the messenger.

The preacher's use of volume should support content. Whether volume should be high or low is dependent on what is being said. Emphasizing a point, a phrase, or a word may call for high volume. High volume should not be used on the less important points, phrases, or words of the sermon. Volume should vary as content varies.

The preacher's use of rate should support content. Rapid rate is usually used when speaking of something familiar to the congregation. Slower rate is used in conjunction with volume to make an emphasis. Some speech experts say the average rate of speech in America varies from 125-150 words per minute. The preacher should determine his own rate of speech and then vary that rate as content dictates.

The preacher's use of pitch should support content. Pitch, for intonation, or inflections have many variations. Higher pitch at the end of a sentence generally suggests that a question is being asked. Lower pitch communicates a serious or somber mood. Higher pitch at the beginning of a sentence communicates a change in mood or thought.

The preacher's use of pauses should support content. Pauses vary in length from a second or less to several seconds. The brief pauses are used to signal the end of a sentence and to maintain a steady flow of thought. The longer pauses are used to allow the congregation to process that which they have just heard or to build suspense before an important pronouncement.

The preacher should take a tape of a previous sermon, transcribe at least two paragraphs, and then listen to the tape while looking at the words. The preacher should critically ask himself some leading questions, such as 'Why did I yell here?' 'Did yelling here support content?' 'Why did I slow down or speed up here?' 'Did the change in rate support content?'

Body Language

We communicate not only with our voices, but with our entire bodies. To focus our discussion, let's concentrate on three areas: posture, gestures and facial expressions.

Posture should be neither rigid nor slouchy. The main area of concern is foot work. When the message to be communicated calls for a sense of urgency, the preacher should place one foot slightly in front of the other and weight should be placed on the forward foot. This makes the preacher's body lean toward the congregation slightly. This bodily posture communicates a sense of urgency. When weight is placed on the back foot, the preacher communicates a sense of withdrawal or rejection. These movements tell the congregation how the preacher and therefore they should feel about what is being said.

Gestures need to be made firmly but gently. Gestures made too firmly will be choppy. Gestures made too gently will be vague and incomplete. The only standard gestures are palms up for acceptance and palms down for rejection. After that, each preacher is free to express himself with any gesture that gives support to content. Wide sweeping gestures, for example, make the entire congregation feel involved. Hands and arms close together communicates a sense of limitation. When making gestures, be sure not to pin your elbows closely to your sides. This limits gestures and makes them ineffective.

Facial expressions are the most individual of all. Basically, the preacher should remember to smile, or to at least look pleasant when speaking of love or joy, and to frown when speaking of sin. Too many preachers frown when they speak of love and smile when they speak of sin. Their facial expressions belie that which they intended to communicate.

Articulate

Articulation refers to the formation of individual sounds which form a word. (Enunciation refers to the overall quality of speech. Pronunciation refers to where the emphasis is placed in a word.) There are three primary articulation problems: substitution of sounds, addition of sounds, and elimination of sounds.

Substitution of sounds is largely a lazy speech habit. The preacher should remember that articulation is to sermon delivery what spelling is to writing. The words just, get, for, because, many and our are often misarticulated as "jist," "git," "fer," "becuz," "mini," "r". Practice saying these words both ways. You will notice quickly that misarticulating these words is simply a lazy way to talk.

Sometimes we add sounds. This, too, is usually done in lazy speech. The words wash and Washington are frequently misarticulated as "warsh" and "Warshington."

The dropping of sounds is the final lazy speech habit. This usually occurs at the end of -ing words: "preachin'," "baptizin'," "eatin'".

Many so-called articulation problems may simply be regional accents. We must all be alert to different accents as we preach in different parts of the world. It would be silly, for instance, for someone from Texas to preach a revival message in Michigan and say, "Ya'll shore do talk funny up heah." Remember, when we are in their territory, we have the accent. When they are in our territory, they have the accent.

Oral Interpretation

The reading of the text is important in effectively communicating a revival message. The art of effective oral reading is known as oral interpretation. Essentially, oral interpretation involves the rules of voice and body language just mentioned.

Oral interpretation is both an art and a science. A simple little practice device could help any preacher increase effectiveness in oral interpretation. Simply select any passage of Scripture, read it aloud vocally emphasizing only one word and vocally de-emphasizing the other words. Do this again, but this time vocally emphasize the next word while de-emphasizing the other words.

For example, let's work through John 2:5, "and Mary said, 'Whatsoever He says to do, you do it.'" Read the sentence aloud, emphasizing the first word. The oral interpretation should have sounded awkward because "And" is not an important word in the sentence. Now read the verse aloud again emphasizing the next word while de-emphasizing the other words. (and *Mary* said, whatsoever he says to do, you do it.) By now you should have a feel for how oral interpretation can help the congregation sense what is important, what is being communicated in the verse. The same exercise can be used with any passage of Scripture.

Spurgeon once said that it is the text and not the sermon that often brings the sinner to a time of conviction. If that is true, then oral interpretation is absolutely necessary to effectively communicating a revival sermon.

Each of the communicative techniques is important. How terrible it would be to prepare a biblically based, clear revival message and to deliver it in such a way that no one feels inclined to make a positive response. While the congregation's attention should never be focused on the preacher's delivery, it will be if the preacher does not focus on effective delivery.

Al Fasol is the E. Hermond Westmoreland Professor of Preaching at Southwestern Baptist Theological Seminary in Fort Worth, Texas.

Preparing to Reach the Lost

Is it possible that all of Christian ministry can be summed up in a single word? More importantly, is it possible that the work of Jesus, from Heaven's introduction to His return to the Father's house can be summed up in a word? The answer is "yes". When Jesus leaves Glory to come to earth, the target is central in everything He said and everything that He did. In all preparation for revival meetings, it has to center first of all, upon this target. There are two Scriptures which introduce this single word, divinely imprinted, Holy Spirit blessed. The first of these Scriptures introduces the word, and the second makes explicit its meaning.

In Luke 19:1-10 is found the familiar story of Jesus and Zacchaeus.

> Jesus entered and passed through Jericho, and behold, there was a man named Zacchaeus which was chief among the Publicans. He was rich. He sought to see Jesus who He was. And could not for the press, because he was little of stature. He ran before and climbed up into a sycamore tree to see him; for he was to pass that way. And when Jesus came to the place, He looked up and saw him and said unto him, 'Zacchaeus, make haste and come down, for today

I must abide at thy house.' And he made haste and came down and received him joyfully. And when they saw it they all murmured saying that he was going to be guest with a man that is a sinner. And Zacchaeus stood and said unto the Lord, behold Lord, the half of my goods I give to feeding the poor; if I have taken anything from any man by false accusation I restore him fourfold. And Jesus said unto him, 'This day has salvation come unto this house, for so much as he also is the son of Abraham. For the Son of Man is come to seek and to save that which was lost.

The theological dimensions, the explicit meaning of the word, is found best in Paul's letter to the church in Ephesus 2:11, 12.

Wherefore remember, that ye being in time past Gentiles in the flesh which are called uncircumcision by that which is called circumcision in the flesh; that at that time you were without Christ, being aliens from the commonwealth of Israel, strangers from the covenant of promise, having no hope without God in the world; but now in Christ Jesus, ye who sometimes were far off are made neigh by the blood of Christ.

How lost is loss? Do you know? How lost is lost? This is a strange word which the Bible uses to describe the Christless life. A pastor with whom I was sharing revival meeting privileges said to me one evening after the service, "I wished we had some other word than the word 'lost.'" I was amazed.

I said to him, "What do you mean?"

He said, "To speak of people being lost, like a lost coin, lost sheep, lost son, what does it mean?"

The heart break of God is in this word. This is not man's word. This is not the preacher's idea. This is not a bit of graphic description. This is not a new promotion. This is God's estimate of a man, a woman that is without Jesus. To be lost is to be lost.

Jesus said to Zacchaeus, "The Son of Man is come to seek and to save that which was lost." The Living Bible version would have this word an adjective, a modifier. It would read "this man also is a lost son of Abraham." Not so! The word stands nakedly alone in the Scripture. It embraces the whole world. There is no modifier that can lend dimension to this word.

In the Old Book, Ezekiel spoke for God to the shepherds of Israel saying "neither have ye sought that which is lost." Later in the same chapter he said "I will seek that which was lost."

Every Christian knows that he was once lost. You can not be a Christian without knowing that you are lost. It is just impossible for you to repent of your sins and come to Christ in faith without an understanding that you are away from God. The knowledge that you are lost is the work of God in our heart, and a work of God in our life. This is the evidence of the convicting work of the Holy Spirit.

What does it mean to you to say that the person sitting next to you is lost, to say that the person to whom you preach is lost, to say more personally that your brother or your son is lost? What does it mean to you to say that your husband is lost? What does it do to you? There is heartbreak in the word, there is *Pathos* in the Word. Seldom when I use it do I see someone weak or someone who seems unusually disturbed. What does it really mean? You cannot basically prepare to seek the lost unless you know how lost is lost.

In Luke's Gospel, the Gospel of Tragedy, he tells the story of a man who had a hundred sheep. One of them is lost. He left the ninety-nine safe in the fold and went out and searched for the lost. He searched until he found it, when he found it he put the sheep upon his shoulders, carried it back to the fold, called in his neighbors and said, "Rejoice with me, that this which was lost is found (Luke 15:4-6)."

He also recounts the story of a woman who had ten coins and one was lost. It was heavy and it fell and rolled. She searched for it and did not find it. She lit a lamp and sought for the coin and did not find it. She swept the house diligently. She searched until she found it. When she found it she called her neighbors and said, "Rejoice with me, that which was lost is found (Luke 15:8-9)."

Finally, in that familiar passage we call the Prodigal Son, he tells us of a man that had two sons.

> The younger of them said, 'Father, give me what is mine.' The father divided unto him his living. Not many days after, the son took his journey into a far country. There he wasted his substance in riotous living.
>
> There arose a mighty famine in the land and he began to be in want. He joined himself unto a citizen of the land, was sent out into

the hog pen to feed swine. He filled his belly with the husks that the swine did eat. No man gave unto him. He came to himself and said, "How many hired servants of my father has plenty and to spare, and I perish with hunger. I will arise and go to my father and say, "Father, I have sinned against Heaven and against thee. I am not worthy to be called thy son. Make we as one of the hired servants."

He arose and went and while he was yet a great way off his father saw him, had compassion on him, ran to meet him, fell on his neck and kissed him. The son sobbed out his confession of sin against Heaven and against his father. The father said, "Bring out the robe and put it on him. Put shoes on his feet. Bring the ring and put it on his finger. Kill the fatted calf. Let us eat and be merry. This my son was lost and is found, he was dead and he is alive (Luke 15:11-24)."

You remember that the elder brother would not come in to share in the rejoicing. The father's plea to him was "thy brother was lost and now he is found. Come in and rejoice with us." What does it mean to you to say that a man is lost, that in a place like that which you occupy, in a privileged circle of life that belongs to you, in the midst of beauty, of peace, or assurance, there is a multitude that is lost?

I have often reminded myself in ministry that on every opportunity given to speak, someone sits there who is a stranger to Jesus, who is lost and waiting to be found. Yet that conviction must be personal. I am persuaded that I cannot pray like I ought to pray, unless I know how lost is lost. You will not visit like a minister ought to visit, unless you know how lost is lost. We cannot even sing like we ought to sing, unless we know the answer to how lost is lost. We cannot exercise the privileges of stewardship, unless in that stewardship we have discovered first, that we were lost and were found. What does it mean to be lost?

I think the best answer to be found in this Book is found in theological terms in the Ephesian Letter. The state of lostness is outlined in simple terms.

First, a man that is lost is *without Christ.* His is a Christless life. Let me put it just as simply as I can. If you have Jesus, you are safe. If you do not have Him, you are lost. If Jesus is in your life and is your Savior, you are a child of God. If He is not in your life, you are lost and have no fellowship with God. You are cut off from God. You are without Christ. That is the word in Ephesians

2:12. It means a Christless life, apart from the Son of God, separated from the Savior, knowing not the Revelation of God which is in Christ Jesus.

What does it mean to be lost? He says that we are "aliens from the commonwealth of Israel." Now, of course, this means spiritual Israel. It is, therefore, the kingdom of God. The idea of being an alien is that of being a stranger in contrast with one who has a home. If you are lost, you are not at home in God's sovereignty because you have not accepted His sovereignty, you have not bowed the knee to God, you have not yielded the heart in faith and devotion. You are a rebel against the government of God. You are not at home in His kingdom. It means you are without the right of citizenship, you are not entitled to the protection of the kingdom of God. You are not in step with the purpose of the kingdom of God, "alien to the commonwealth of Israel."

Scripture continues that the person who is lost is "a stranger to the covenant of promise." Certainly, this means first that a person is a foreigner to a covenant by having no share in it. All of the promises in our Bible concerning the Savior mean nothing when you are lost. All of the wonderful words in this Book about the purchase Jesus made for us on Calvary mean nothing because we are lost and away from God.

Every week I am confronted with the promises of God in public service, often in a funeral service. Those promises mean nothing to the individual that is without Jesus. The summary word in this Scripture is *"having no hope."* I know no sadder words in the language than "no hope." I have heard them many times through the years about the physical distresses of life. I have heard the doctor say those words many times about someone in whom I had an investment of love, because they were my people. There was no hope.

On the human side of the equation this is to establish the desperate dimension of being lost. The time ticked away, and the days went by and suddenly, the hopelessness became apparent to all. No hope is a far more serious thing to say about a soul "without hope." That means no hope in time, in eternity, anywhere, for the life that is without Jesus. He is lost. There is no personal preparation to seek the lost until the enormity, the desperate hopelessness of that condition is a personal conviction.

All of this is put together in a summary word "without God in this world." You may go out in the beauty of a dawning morning of the Spring, and see the handiwork of God, and know the beauty that is there. But, you will not know God. You are without God if you are lost. You may believe, convinced by that which is mysterious evidence of His presence in the world, you may believe that God is; but you are without hope if you are lost. How terrible is the state of the lost.

So I come back to the basic question, the essential element in personal preparation for seeking the lost, to ask my own heart and yours, *how lost is lost?*

The first answer must be lost enough to bring Jesus from Heaven's glory to earth's poverty to seek Zacchaeus, to seek me, to seek you until He finds us. I believe that God teaches plainly in His Book that Jesus left Heaven to come into this world to search for me, to find me, a lost sinner, and to die for me on Calvary's tree.

I write these words about preparing to reach the lost and suddenly confront this basic mystery. We can be sure that God has told us all that we are capable of knowing about the preparation of the Savior to come to earth. As He was later to share with His disciples about a cross that waited for Him, He must have shared with that Heavenly Host that surrounded Him His intent to come for us. The Scriptures actually give us a brief look at the angels who are amazed at the spectacle of His departure. The putting aside of the robes of His divinity, that He might walk among men and women who are lost, is in itself a staggering concept. To say that Jesus, the Son of God, becomes a babe in Bethlehem's stall is a journey for the lost.

Did you ever try to tell anybody about Jesus who had never heard His name? I have often asked missionaries for an explanation of the dilemma, for the moment of dawning that comes to the lost. I am confident that the miracle there is the miracle here.

A preparation to reach the lost must began at the beginning. What do you say first? You begin to tell them about a rich tax collector of two millenniums ago who came face to face with the Son of God. When he spoke of that which he did in terms of good works, he was told by the Savior that He had come to seek and to save that which was lost. The Spirit, the searching Spirit, suddenly brings this tax collector to know that he is lost, that he is the object of the search, that there is hope for him to walk in fellowship with God.

It seems to me that Jesus would have said in addition to Zacchaeus, "Come down. I have been looking for you. From the infinity that was mine in eternity and from the presence of the Godhead, and from the presence and love and devotion of the angels, I have been searching for you. Before flesh had brought you to identity in this world, I was searching for you with the redeeming love of God. Come down Zacchaeus, I have an appointment with you. I have been looking for you."

Suddenly, he is not just a tax collector. He may be a cheating, thieving tax collector. It matters not. Jesus has come to save him. There are the others of the same pattern, having the same need, feeling the same lostness. Bartimeaus, crying from the wayside on the road out of Jerusalem is one of them. Jesus said,"Bring him to me." So they brought him, this blind man, to an appointment with the Son of God. God sent His Son from Glory to seek, to search, and to find a blind man that was lost, crying out on the fringes.

"Jesus, thou Son of David, have mercy on me." The people about Him did not understand.

They said, "Be still, he has no time for you. Can you not see that He is extremely busy in the presence of the multitudes?"

Yet he continues to cry. This is his day of appointment. The Son of God has come for him. All of the preparation to seek vocalizes into the search for one.

There is a woman who approaches Him as He sits by the well. She has partial knowledge. Against that background, Jesus said to her, "I that speak unto thee am He," and suddenly, it is the lost and the Savior. Suddenly, that which is lost is found. The target that was so clear in the outset is so emphatically outlined in its accomplishment. The Son of Man is come to seek and to save that which is lost.

We prepare to seek the lost when we realize that is the *whole mission* of our Lord. Without understanding that, we will never really seek the lost. We can establish programs, we can order exercises, we can make appeals, but the basic truth is that this person is lost, that Jesus came and died for him and lives to save him. The basic truth is that you and I are simply witnesses to that which has happened to us when He said to us, "I have been looking for you. I came from Eternity for you."

It is so fitting that the concluding chapter of that earthly ministry is in the same vein. A thief dying by His side makes the appeal "Lord, remember me when thou comest into thy Kingdom." Remember him! Jesus said to him, "This day thou shall be with me in Paradise." From the cross, that becomes my hope and redeeming price, He bears one that He has just found, even in dying, into the presence of the Father.

How lost is lost? We are never prepared for witnessing until we answer. A second answer must well be 'Lost enough to bring Jesus from Heaven to earth for us, and lost enough to keep Him *steadily on course to the cross.'* He told His disciples that He had come to die. No Scripture is more pointed than that which says "He set His face steadfastly toward Jerusalem." The cost was a reality to Him in the outset. Jesus came to die. Yet as the road grows more difficult, as the hill becomes steeper, as the price becomes obvious to people like us, we can well understand that this is the crux of the search.

How could He press on to the cross, when a single word would have put the cross aside. How could He give himself into the hands of violent men who would extract His blood, when by a word, they would have fallen at his feet. The wonderful mystery is that without the death itself, that which was lost would never have been found. The ultimate hope of the sinner is that the sacrifice was made on our behalf.

It is essential that beyond all else, that in preparing to reach the lost, one finds in his own heart an understanding of the miracle, of the mystery, of the dimension of Calvary itself. Jesus advanced steadily toward the cross. We are familiar with the scene that surrounded the day we call Easter. The pictures of the pilgrims repeating the journey to the cross fill our television screens. Our sermons center upon the last of this ultimate journey. It is properly so. Can I answer the question, how lost is lost and make you understand that it is that lostness of that individual who looks so familiar that finally brings Jesus to say, "It is finished. Into Thy hands I commit my spirit." Suddenly, there is victory and in the midst of the saddest scene, hope springs eternal.

It follows logically enough when we ask how lost is lost to say, lost enough to be worth any sacrifice. We talk about preparing to reach the lost, no one is prepared as simply an added activity. It must become the priority. It must become the only driving force in life. It must never raise a question as to cost. We are only prepared to seek the lost when it becomes the ultimate joy, the driving force, the goal indeed, of every breath.

We are familiar with he fact that life is given to us in unequal portions. Suffering for one is not suffering for another. Sacrifice in one life is not the same as sacrifice in another life.

The sum total of all of that is to say that there is nothing in life that is as important as the privilege of bearing witness to the finding, saving, blood-cleansing power of God. To say this is to allow us to establish our standards of measurement for our readiness for the task. We must remember first that we ourselves were lost, and the joy that we had when we were found. It never grows commonplace. It becomes life's chief miracle in our own heart. We do not need to turn to another to ask what is this. We have only to look in our own life to understand God's ultimate love, God's total concern, God's triumphant victory.

Bolstered by that memory, made strong by that present strengthening of the Spirit, we join in the search. There is no uncertainty about the steps, there is no lack of appreciation for its urgency, for we know how desperate is the state of which they speak when they say "this man is lost." Urgency always characterizes the Christian enterprise, not because we need results; that is not even a word of consideration. The urgency lies in the lostness and the hope that is in Jesus. We can only count ourselves prepared to seek the lost when it is the chief priority of life.

Robert E. Naylor is President Emeritus of Southwestern Baptist Theological Seminary in Fort Worth, Texas, having served as President from 1958 to 1978.

PREPARING FOR A REVIVAL MEETING BY BECOMING A SERVANT IN THE PULPIT

Here's to the minister of the church! See him or her as the double servant: the servant of God and the servant of the people. We have developed too singular and narrow a use of the word "minister." For most the word simply means "preacher". At other moments it is used as a synonym for the word "reverend" or "pastor". In Scripture the word was never meant for narrow use. If there are 500 members in any particular church there ought to be 500 ministers and servants. Jesus said that the greatest member of any church is the one who most serves (Matt. 20:25-28).

The church is ever in danger of forgetting how to minister. Yet there is no end to need. People are constantly around us who are ill or need some errand run. There are also the lonely who need the friendship of Christ to bring confidence to their lives. What is the church doing about all these needs? Often nothing! The very moment you were born-again, you were commissioned a servant in the Kingdom of God.

I am intrigued and often convicted by ancient parables. Once on a dangerous seacoast where shipwrecks often occurred, there was a crude, small, life-saving station. The building was just a hut and so poor it owned only one rescue boat. Still the few devoted members of the station kept a constant watch over the sea, and, with no thought for themselves, they lived day and night searching for the lost. Indeed, they were most effective. So many lives were saved by this wonderful little station that it became famous. Some of those who had been rescued were so grateful they wanted to become associated with the little station and give of their time, effort and money for the support of the work. Thus the work expanded. New boats were bought and new crews were trained as the life-saving station continued to grow. The ardor they spent in lives of rescue gave them a sense of their importance and their place in the world.

Still as time went on, some of the members of the life-saving station became despondent because the little station was so crude and poorly equipped. They felt that a more comfortable place should be provided as the first refuge of those saved from the sea. They sacrificed their livings and out of that sacrifice grew a new building in the same spirit of sacrifice and courage with which they served the rescue operation. When the new station was complete they replaced the tattered cots with real beds. They also put better furniture in the newly enlarged facility. The splendid new station gained class and became a popular gathering place for all the rescuers. The members decorated it beautifully and furnished it exquisitely. It was so popular it became a sort of "Rescue Club." Now, however, fewer members were interested in going out into the sea on life-saving maneuvers. It was cold, nasty, wet work. So they decided to open up new classes on how to rescue the drowning. They had advanced classes on how to toss a ring buoy and the famous "chin pry" back stroke in perilous waters. There were so many classes to be taught they really had very little time to become really engaged in the actual work. So instead of going out themselves they hired life-boat crews to do the rescuing.

Not long after the building of the exquisite new rescue club a large ship was wrecked off the coast. The hired crews worked tirelessly bringing in loads of cold, wet, and half-drowned people. They came in dirty and sick, dripping sea-water on all the new carpets. The beautiful new rescue club was stained and very unkempt. So the property committee immediately had a shower house built outside the lovely new rescue club, where the shipwrecked victims could be hosed down and cleaned up before being brought inside.

At the next meeting there was a split at the business meeting of the club. Most of the members wanted to stop the life-saving activities. They saw the actual rescue work as a hinderance to the normal social life of the club. Some of the members insisted that life-saving was the primary purpose and pointed out that they were still called a "life-saving station". But they were considered dissidents and voted down. These dissidents were told very simply that if they wanted to save lives of all the various kinds of people who were being shipwrecked, they would have to begin their own life-saving station somewhere down the coast.

They did. It was a poor little station with only one boat but it did a remarkable job of rescue.

As the years went by, the new station experienced the same changes that had occurred in the old. While it began to save the desperate, it soon evolved into another elite club, which, like its predecessor, soon experienced a club split and yet another life-saving station was founded somewhat further down the coast. History continued to repeat itself, and, if you were to visit that sea coast today, you would find a number of exclusive clubs along that shore. Shipwrecks are still frequent in those waters, but now most of the people drown.[1]

Lord:

Does it mean Saviour or Servant?

Does it mean Prince or Peasant?

Jesus was both but let us assume that the Lord of the church and the servant of humanity is the same person, Jesus.

If Lord is the first word of each new believer, servant is the second. Just as the child nearly always had for his first word the word "Mamma" or "Dadda", perhaps it is true that our first word in our pilgrimage of faith is the word "Lord".

Indeed, it is this word which makes a man Christian, just as it is the phrase "I do" which makes a man into a husband or a woman into a wife.

Of course, it is natural, when a couple stands at the altar and says "I do" they have just become husband and wife. Were one of them to break the rules of anticipation and say, "No", or "I suppose" no union could occur.

What is there in the "I doing" of marriage vows that makes a Miss and a Mister into a Mr. and Mrs.? There is a sense of commitment. Any person not ready to get down to business of marriage had better not say "I do", for beyond those two syllables of consent is a lifetime of obligation.

The moment you call Christ "Lord", you call yourself "Servant". The moment you say in sincerity "King Jesus" you call yourself "Subject". There is fickleness in human nature. Sometimes a man who pledges himself to the service of the United States Army goes A.W.O.L. Reno, Nevada is proof that not everyone who says "I do" does. Not everyone pledges allegiance to the flag is a good American. Not everyone who takes a jurors' oath tells the truth, the whole truth, and nothing but the truth. Some of those who promise to love, honor, and obey, hate, dishonor and disregard those to whom they have promised.

But nowhere is the fickle nature of man more obvious than in church. A million, or ten million, have called Christ "Lord" without meaning it. Lord, has become a common word, a weak synonym for God, a "Sunday-go-to-meeting" word. You may use the word "Lord" a lot and only mean it a little, but keep in mind the admonition of Jesus:

> Not everyone that sayeth unto me "Lord, Lord" shall enter into the kingdom of heaven; but he that doeth the will of my Father which is in heaven. (Matthew 7:21)

Let us look at what the scripture teaches about the Lordship of Jesus Christ.

> And he said unto her, What wilt Thou? She saith unto him, Grant that these my two sons may sit, the one on thy right hand, and the other on the left, in thy kingdom. (Matthew 20:21)

James and John talk to Jesus just like most people today talk to him . . . "Lord, listen here, make us great . . . !" They could say "Lord" in such a condescending way it sounded like "bellman, the tip is under the luggage."

How often we are told what God can do *for* us; how rarely what God can do *with* us. God, no longer the cosmic policeman of the fiery furnace religion, is now seen as a cosmic valet, ready to do anything to make life pleasant and save us at a bargain price never asking for anything in return. In the Old Testament days, as you remember, Samuel prayed, "Speak, Lord, for thy servant heareth (I Samuel 3:10)." But, how many pray today, "Listen, Lord, for thy servant speaketh. Thou must give unto me a good job, a nice family, a fine set of principles with the accent on flexibility, of course, and most of all, peace, O Lord, a peace that nothing can disturb." Occasionally this type of prayer has a P.S., "Oh, yes, Lord, I have done wrong. No need to forgive me. Just don't let anyone find out. And one more thing, help me to gather enough reputation as I pass along so that I can keep my self-esteem."[2]

James and John were really saying, "Christ, don't forget you are the servant, and you can best serve us by making us lords." In effect, most of our praying for servanthood like theirs really means, "I want to be Lord rather than have a Lord."

The Servant Species

II Corinthians 5:17 says, "Therefore if any man be in Christ, he is a new creature. Old things are passed away, behold, all things become new."

Really what this verse teaches is that each Christian is a member of the servant species. We ought to celebrate his Lordship as that which makes us a continual species.

> Monkeys have been removed from their mothers by Caesarian section, raised without contact with other monkeys, and then placed in a cage with one side a rear-projection screen. On this screen will be projected pictures and movies of children, landscapes, and animals. All of these drew only a "ho-hum" from the monkey; but flash a picture of another monkey on that screen and instantly, the captive, who has never seen one of his own kind, reacts excitedly, trying to get through to that other monkey. Cognition of one's species seems to be genetic in the higher mammals.[3]

Christians ought to recognize each other from their common slavery. They are servants.

Now, you cannot have a Lord and be a Lord at the same time. That's our frustration in the church. A life, like an automobile, can have only one in control. Two people trying to drive the same car will end up badly. As long as you seek to control your own life while pretending to give it to Christ will cause it to end badly.

Christ's number one question to us is, "CAN YOU CALL ME LORD? Can you drink the cup that I drink of . . ."

Look at the interplay of 'you' and 'I' in these verses.

"You know not what ye ask: can ye drink of the cup that I drink of? and be baptized with the baptism that I am baptized with? (Mark 10:38)"

James and John came to Jesus asking to be made lords. Jesus tells them that they seek too much and that they should be seeking that special servant relationship. Then Christ goes on to remind them that although they and the rest of the world should call him, "Lord", he has really come as a servant. He will serve humanity washing feet. He will serve the sick by healing them. He will serve the lonely by being a friend. He will serve the lost by dying on the cross. So, if he, the Lord of Christianity was Servant, how much more ought they to be his followers. They will serve him, but much more, they will personally serve for they are personal servants.

Above this there is no question: Christ demands obedience!

Elizabeth Elliot Leach tells about her young brother Tom. When he was very young he used to take sacks and use them for stepping stones around the kitchen. One day his mother said, "Tommy, pick them up!" Mr. Howard, Tommy's father, was playing the piano and little Tommy said, "I want to sing Jesus Loves Me!" Tommy, to obey is better than sacrifice. (I Samuel 15:22) Young Tom Howard seems to have had the same affliction from which many Christians suffer. It's a lot more pleasing to talk about how much we love God rather than simply obey Him.

We all have this feeling that the church is the center to love and receive love. But the church is the obedience center of the Kingdom. There is a "deeper life" movement where everybody wants to sit around and just love God. But that has never been the commandment of the church.

Suppose you tell your little boy to take out the trash and he answers this way:

"Dad, I just want to contemplate the beauty of your face."

"Son, Take out the trash."

"Oh, Dad, I love you so much . . ."

"SON, TAKE OUT THE TRASH!"

To obey is better than sacrifice. Until you learn to obey you have not and can not see the glory of the Lordship of Christ. Some would say that the church has now produced only a servanthood of sterility. We serve, but there is something cold and clinical about it all.

I think I understand the death that exists in the average evangelical church. I went to a church quite recently where I sensed the sterility of the product. All that they said was correct. There was no doctrinal fault among them. But they didn't see their immediate world.

Conclusion

Do you want to be Lord of your life? Lord of your petty affairs? Verse 45 . . . Even Jesus became a servant for you. Will you become a servant for him? Can you truly say "Lord Jesus"? Still it is no good just to say it. You must mean it, too.

Do you know how to be the greatest man or woman in your church? Don't try to get elected to some office. Be a servant to Jesus. Help your church find some way to get Christ out of your church and into the streets of your hometown. They don't need to come to the church, not primarily. They don't need to go to anybody's church. They need Christ . . . in their homes, in their companies, in their lives.

Bishop Kennedy once told of a little old woman who lived absolutely friendless and alone. She died in her apartment and it was a few days before anyone found her. As they leafed through her diary they found on the last page of each day that she was alive that she had written, "Nobody came to call on me today."

When I first went to Kansas City in 1958, a young girl was fished out of the muddy Missouri River with a faded suicide note pinned to her blouse; "I haven't a friend in the world, nobody cares for me."

Where were the Baptist churches during these incidences? Wrapped up in administration? Arguing in their business meetings? Planning spaghetti suppers? Studying mission books? And the pastor was trying to untangle hurt feelings and bad politics within the church.

Recently, as a pastor friend of mine was about to go on Christmas vacation. An odd and wrenching occurrence almost detained him. A little couple visited his church and asked him to call on them. He planned to get it done before he left for Christmas. Still, he had in his membership one of those cantankerous superintendents of something or other who was demanding his time because the work of the church needed to be done. So, he ignored the petition of the needy couple and spent nearly every night in the home of this "troubled church member." Hastily he went by the home of the couple who had pled for his help. But the afternoon when he went they were not in. He left his card and then he left for the holidays.

After the pastor left one of his members called me and asked me for his home address. The couple that had so needed him and had come to the church out of desperation were found in tragic circumstances. The man had been found in a car, his head blown off with a shotgun. He had taken his own life. When they went to tell his wife they found that before he had killed himself, he had killed her. She was dead.

When the pastor found out about their tragic deaths, his eyes filled with tears. I could tell that he was thinking about that busy, hyper-active church member who had taken so much of his time that he never got to see the desperate souls who were begging his help.

Someone in this world needs your love. Some home needs Christ. He is the Answer to fulfillment and meaning and you are the servant—his servant . . . either that or you don't matter.

Endnotes

1. Theodore O. Wedel, *The Ecumenical Review,* Vol. VI, October 1953.

2. William Sloan Coffin, Jr., *The Call,* Sermon taken from *Sermons To Intellectuals,* Edited by Franklin H. Littell (New York: The Macmillan Company, 1963) pp. 10-11.

3. J.C. Pearce, *Exploring The Crack In The Cosmic Egg* (New York: Pocket Books, 1975) p. 65.

Calvin Miller is Professor of Communication and Ministry Studies and Writer in Residence at Southwestern Baptist Theological Seminary, Fort Worth, Texas.

Preparing for Invitations in a Revival Meeting

The word "invitation" in nontheological language is one which is easily understood. People understand what it means to invite someone over for a visit or to ask someone to accompany them on a picnic or a trip. In theological or evangelical terms the invitation is an appeal to someone to accept the benefits of the Christian gospel. These benefits are numerous; they include forgiveness of sin, a new quality of life, peace, purpose, life everlasting, and many more. Since these benefits come through a Person, an evangelistic invitation is an appeal to accept this Person, Jesus Christ, into one's life as Savior and Lord.

Assuming that the conditions for receiving salvation have been clearly set forth, the invitation as here discussed, will be an appeal to people to meet these conditions and to openly demonstrate their willingness to do so by taking some specific action which will be prescribed by the preacher. Generally this action will be coming forward to the front of the auditorium as indication that one is receiving Christ. I am convinced that every minister of the gospel can learn how to give a good invitation. Every preacher might not have the ability which would make him a great preacher, but almost without exception each one can give a strong invitation. It is something which can be learned.

Reasons for Giving an Invitation

I. The Nature of the Gospel

When one studies the message of apostolic preachers, the conclusion becomes obvious that one distinction of New Testament preaching was that preaching and invitation were virtually inseparable. The very nature of the message they preached compelled them to appeal for response.

The gospel message is of such a nature that an invitation to response is the logical outcome of its declaration. After his sermon at Pentecost, Peter called on his hearers to repent and be baptized (Acts 2:38). After his second recorded sermon, his imperative was: "Repent ye therefore, and be converted, that your sins may be blotted out" (Acts 3:19).

Jesus frequently coupled the indicative and the imperative. He would conclude a message with "Except ye repent, ye shall all likewise perish" (Luke 13:3), or "Repent ye, and believe the gospel" (Mark 1: 15). God makes man a concrete offer of forgiveness of sin on the basis of the saving acts of his Son. Such an offer demands a decision. The good news of Jesus is of such a nature that it demands a verdict. To refuse to urge someone to respond to the gospel would be similar to a salesman who, after eloquently describing his product and his benefits, leaves you without even inviting you to purchase it.

II. The Nature of Man Calls for an Invitation

By his very makeup, man needs the opportunity to respond to the gospel. Someone has well said that "impression without expression can lead to depression." To preach for response and to fail to provide an opportunity for a commitment can frustrate those who hear the gospel and deepen them in their habit of procrastination.

III. Invitations Are Biblical

From beginning to end, invitations are extended in Scripture. God's probing question to Adam in the garden, "Where art thou?"

in Genesis 3 is something of an invitation. The final chapter of the Bible contains an invitation, "And the Spirit and the bride say, Come. And let him that heareth say, Come. And let him that is athirst come. And whosoever will, let him take the water of life freely" (Rev. 22:17).

IV. The Testimony of Evangelical History

The invitation certainly has its historic evangelical basis. That is, through much of evangelical church history, there has been an immediate appeal on the part of preachers to their congregations to respond to the gospel. Churches of various faiths, which are evangelistically inclined, usually make some kind of appeal for people to register a commitment to Christ or interest in making such a commitment.

V. Some Will Decide for Christ

Because of public invitation, some people will decide for Christ who would not have otherwise decided. Admittedly, in asking for public commitments, there is the danger of premature response. But this must be balanced against the possibility that failure to give opportunity for decision may keep many from making a decision for which they are ready. After the good news has been preached, many who hear are ready to openly commit themselves. The old adage, "Strike while the iron is hot," is not inappropriate here. Impression without expression can lead to depression and can result in a person's turning away from the gospel once and for all.

VI. Invitations Are Psychologically Sound

There is a psychological soundness in giving opportunity for public response. Making a public commitment has a way of putting strength and fiber in a decision made privately in the heart. It is like driving down a spiritual stake that can amount to saying, "I'm burning bridges behind me, I'm cutting cables once and for all; I'm taking my stand for Christ and for right." There is psychological soundness in coming forward. It is a strengthening factor to men to give them opportunities to openly declare what they're doing in their hearts.

How to Give an Invitation

I. Give the Invitation with a Spiritually Prepared Mind

Many of us extend invitations without ever giving serious consideration to the issues which are at stake. There is an awesome aspect to confronting an individual or a congregation with the offer of the Christian gospel. Every soul to whom we present the claims of Christ is an eternity bound person. Their decision about what we offer could and ultimately will affect their eternal destiny. The choice which will mean heaven or hell is made for many during the period of public invitation. But there is more involved than eternal destinies. The benefits of the good news are experienced not only in the sweet by-and-by but in the ugly here and now as well. Jesus can put the pieces of broken lives together again. Peace, joy, purpose, removal of guilt: all are benefits which can be known by those who make an affirmative response to Christ. The mind of the one offering the invitation should be saturated with these facts before offering it.

II. Extend the Invitation Confidently and Expectantly

Every message should be preached and every invitation extended in the confidence that God wants things to happen. Many times, what happens when we invite people to Christ depends on what we expect to happen. As Jesus was unable to do mighty works at Nazareth because of their unbelief, so in our invitations is he unable to do mighty works because we do not believe.

III. Give the Invitation Dependently

Real transformation of life in an invitation is not dependent on human contrivance, but on the work of the Holy Spirit. He alone can convict of spiritual need. Only he can reveal Christ savingly. He is the only one who can perform the miracle which we call the new birth. Thus, the invitation should be given in dependence on him. The fact that all of this is his work should be wonderful encouragement to us. We are channels through whom he works. Yielded to him we give him opportunity to move in the lives of those to whom we preach.

IV. Give the Invitation Clearly

I marvel at times at the clarity with which Billy Graham extends the invitation. He tells people exactly what he wants them to do and precisely how he wants them to express the fact that they're doing it. He is very explicit in giving his invitation and in specifying the manner in which he wants them to express the fact that they are inviting Christ into their lives.

We should be specific in inviting them to make open and public that commitment. We should spell out precisely what we want people to do. A lack of being specific here can cheapen an evangelistic appeal. In a sense, this subtracts from the luster of the gospel and can open the door of response so wide that almost anyone would have to come forward to maintain a sense of integrity.

V. Give the Invitation Honestly

All of us have been in invitations where the pastor or evangelist has said, "We're going to have one more stanza," and before we know it one has become three or four or five. If ever you have the impression that the invitation should be continued after making such a statement, express your feeling to the congregation. Ask them to forgive you as you retract the statement you made previously, but that you have confidence that they will understand.

VI. Give the Invitation Courteously

The invitation should be given with the love, patience, and gentleness of Christ. This is no time to scold, criticize, berate, chastise, or bully an audience. In my opinion, you will fail for certain in your invitation if you attempt any of these. A true minister of the gospel should remain sensitive to the feelings of people to whom he has been preaching.

There is no place for unnecessary embarrassment of a congregation. Some preachers employ an invitation in which hands are raised, but make the mistake of putting extreme pressure on those who simply raised their hands for prayer. A hand raised for prayer is no excuse for bullying a person down the aisle.

VII. Give the Invitation Thoroughly

This is just another way of saying take adequate time for the invitation. John Bisagno, pastor of First Baptist Church, Houston, has suggested, "I have found that 90 percent of the converts come forward after the third verse of the invitation." Do not he discouraged if there is not immediate response as you make all appeal for Christ. Sometimes it takes more time for the Holy Spirit to do his work.

VIII. Give the Invitation Authoritatively

There is no reason for apology in extending and invitation. We're inviting people to accept a quality of life they could never find anywhere else. The most sensible thing one could do would be to respond to our offer to receive Christ. The invitation should be given authoritatively. I have marveled at times as I have observed Billy Graham extending an invitation. You get the impression that he is almost ordering people to repent and believe. But why shouldn't he and why shouldn't we? We have the authority of heaven behind us when we call men to repentance. A note of authority or lack of it is one of the keys to a successful ministry and one of our worse failures in giving an invitation. As we invite men to break with the old life, a life which to many is a life of degradation, emptiness, and bondage, we are calling them to a life of freedom, forgiveness, and newness in Christ. With authority and without apology it should be done.

IX. Give the Invitation Urgently

If we have any concept at all as to the size of the issues involved, urgency will characterize our invitation. The New Testament says, "Behold, now is the accepted time; behold, now is the day of salvation" (2 Cor. 6:2). Until a man responds affirmatively to Jesus as Savior and Lord, he is living in rebellion against him. People should not be encouraged to leave the service without being brought face to face with their responsibility of responding to Christ. We should not invite them to go away and think over whether they are going to receive him or not.

X. Give the Invitation Smoothly

Many preachers find that making the transition from the sermon to the invitation to be a bit difficult. Because this is a crucial matter, special attention ought to be given to it. It is true that the Spirit of God overrules our mistakes at times and there are unusual results in response to an invitation in spite of our unnecessary clumsiness. On the other hand, a slovenly transition can distract and hinder the Spirit's work. Smooth transition is a matter to be worked out between the preacher, music leader, choir, and accompanists. A system of understood signals between the pastor and the minister of music is a necessity. Regardless of the content of the sermon, through adequate planning its termination point can always be related to the importance of decision for Christ.

Planning Your Invitation

It is difficult to stress too much the importance of the invitation. It is not something merely tacked on to the end of the sermon as an afterthought. The sermon should build toward those all-important moments when people will be asked to decide for Christ. In most services, all that has gone before, the singing, the praying and the sermon, has really been done to make ready for the invitation. Planning is desirable in case there is an unusual response in an invitation. If the invitation is extended for a rather lengthy period, it is a good idea to have the minister of music ready to change the invitation hymn. This should be planned beforehand.

Though most invitations involve an appeal to come forward, there are other types which could be employed with great profit. A preacher should have two or three types of invitations in mind and trust the Holy Spirit to lead him as to which he should use. There are several possibilities.

I. Invitation to Come Forward to Openly Confess Christ

In many evangelistic churches, the standard invitation is an invitation to come to the front in acknowledgment of acceptance of Christ as Lord and Savior. This kind of invitation usually involves a word of counsel with the pastor and remaining at the front in order to be presented to the congregation. To all who employ this kind of invitation, a word of caution is in order. A clear distinction should be made between those who are coming merely as inquirers. It is the opinion of this author that a majority of those who come in response to an evangelistic invitation have not yet had a valid conversion experience when they make their journey from their seat to the front of the auditorium.

Some who come have been led to Christ previously and some have really trusted him during the message or invitation. But many come as "seekers" or as "inquirers" and should be counseled as such. There's a desperate need for more than a handshake with the preacher and the filling out of a card. Failure to counsel with a person under these conditions is alarmingly presumptuous and represents an inexcusably careless dealing with the souls of men. When there is any doubt as to whether or not a person really trusted Jesus, the invitation to come forward should be combined with our opportunity for individual counseling.

II. Invitation to Go to an Inquiry Room for Further Counsel

A second type of invitation which has many advantages is an invitation which makes use of counselors and a counseling room. In this kind of invitation, people would be invited to come forward and either stand in the alter area or leave the auditorium with a counselor during the invitation.

It is my opinion that the pastor cannot do adequate counseling with every person who comes forward in the invitation. This is true if a large number of people come. It is also true if only a small number of people come if each of the small number has particular problems with which one ought to deal.

Because of limited time and opportunity for counsel during the invitation on the pastor's part, every church of any size should have some well-trained counselors to assist the pastor in talking to people who come forward. My personal preference is that this counseling be done outside the auditorium and not be so rushed that it is always necessary to present people to the church in the same service during which they came forward.

III. Invitation to Sign a Card

A third option as to types of invitation would be an invitation for interested people to fill out cards which would be placed in the back of the pews. On the card would be printed a statement of acceptance of Christ, of desire to know more about becoming a Christian, or any other commitment someone in the congregation might be inclined to make. After the message, in a period of meditation, people could be invited to fill in the cards appropriately. After doing this, those who have filled out cards could be asked to take the card with them after the benediction to a clearly designated counseling room.

Some pastors employ cards as a part of the invitation and ask those who have filled them out to leave them in the back of the pew or some other designated place. The pastor would then follow up by making a personal call at their home to speak with them further.

IV. Invitation to Raise One's Hand

In years gone by, a popular kind of invitation was one in which people were invited to raise their hand. When employing this kind of invitation with tact and discretion, it can be of much spiritual benefit to some who are desiring spiritual help. While the congregation is bowed in prayer, invite all who sense their need and want to invite Christ into their lives to simply raise their hands as indication that they are making the decision to do so.

V. Invitation to Pray at One's Seat

Many people who have heard an evangelistic sermon or even an evangelistic appeal would like the opportunity to pray. But, many times they don't know exactly how to pray. The pastor should invite all who want to become Christians to follow him as he leads them in a "sinner's prayer." Having explained, to them that he is going to lead them in a prayer of acceptance of Christ, he should slowly lead them to pray softly or silently after him.

Needless to say, combinations of any of the above suggested methods of invitation are always possible. One might invite people to pray at their seats and to then invite those who have prayed to come forward in public confession of Christ. This combination and a number of others would be possible if one employed the above suggestions.

Exhortation and Invitation

When Peter's sermon at Pentecost pierced the armor of his hearers and struck a responsive chord, the New Testament says, "With many other words did he testify and exhort, saying, Save yourselves from this untoward (crooked) generation." Where the earlier part of his message had been a declaration of facts about Jesus coupled with an imperative to repent, this portion of his message is composed of his urgent appeal to respond to what he has said. It appears that he was giving them good sound reasons why they ought to turn to Jesus.

In extending invitations today, exhortation is still a very viable part of our verbal appeal. Exhortation is a plea for action on the basis of sound reason. There are a number of bases for motivation to action, each of which is consistent with the dignity of the gospel we preach.

I. The Appeal to Self-preservation

Some psychologists have contended that man's strongest instinct is the instinct of self-preservation. What could speak more eloquently to this drive than the message of everlasting life? Some today question the wisdom of appealing to the emotion of fear, either in sermon or invitation. Though this should not be our primary basis of appeal, it is nonsense not to acquaint people with the dangers of spiritual procrastination or indifference.

II. Appeal to the Highest Quality of Life

One of the finest appeals is the appeal to discover the highest quality of life possible. Jesus offers, to needy people, life abundant. Appeal to those in your congregation whose lives are griped by enervating anxiety and fear to exchange these for the peace and joy Jesus can give.

III. Appeal for Recognition and Acceptance

The invitation is a good time to remind individuals that "God knows you and he loves you. What a thrilling privilege to share with people who feel like an unimportant nobody that to God they are an important somebody. He recognizes them as people of worth and accepts them in his Son. This is a worthy appeal in any invitation.

IV. The Appeal to the Yearning for Freedom

Real freedom is not freedom to sin but freedom from sin and its consequences. Freedom comes only from Jesus. There is freedom from sin's guilt, penalty, and fear. He looses man from the fetters of selfishness which put him in bondage. We should appeal to man's longing for real freedom.

V. The Appeal to Fulfillment

Many people who hear us preach sense a real lack of fulfillment in life. They have tried many things for satisfaction only to be left empty after exhausting them all. Those to whom we preach and to whom we appeal during the invitation need to be told that fulfillment will come only as Christ comes into their life. He alone can fill the "God-shaped blank" in every man.

Many other appeals could be made during the invitation: an appeal to adventure in life; an appeal to influence over others; an appeal to Supreme duty; an appeal to gratitude; and an appeal to the need for an intimate friend. Though these lists do not exhaust all possible motives and instincts to which we may appeal, the basic ones are there. Creative ingenuity will aid you to list others and will amplify ways of using the ones listed above.

Invitations are extended to people. Every sensible appeal should be made to lost humanity to receive salvation from Christ. From every legitimate basis the appeal should be made. The invitation to receive Christ should appeal to every human facility possible.

Roy J. Fish is Distinguished Professor of Evangelism and occupant of the L.R. Scarborough Chair of Evangelism at Southwestern Baptist Theological Seminary, Fort Worth, Texas. This chapter is a condensed version of his book, Giving A Good Invitation *and is used here by his permission. The book was condensed into this chapter by Albert L. Harris, a former Graduate Assistant in the Evangelism Department of Southwestern Baptist Theological Seminary and presently Pastor of the Brookwood Baptist Church in Hillsboro, Oregon.*

PREPARING FOR REVIVAL MEETINGS IN A MULTI-CONGREGATIONAL CHURCH

Revival often comes spontaneously. On the otherhand, revivals, in the sense of special times of spiritual reflection and soul-winning emphasis, often follow times of planning and preparation. Whether by a spontaneous movement or following planning and preparation, the results and blessings of revival and revivals spring totally from the power of the Holy Spirit of God. The fact that God sometimes sees fit to bless his churches with times of refreshing and power demands that God's people seek to do those things that often opens the ways to revival.

This chapter explores plans churches and other groups of Christians in multi- congregational churches can do that eventuate in revival. Nothing that will be mentioned can insure nor demand revival. Such preparations have, however, been followed by revival. The multi-congregational church has special needs and opportunities in seeking the Holy Spirit's power for revival. It should be noted that many multi-congregational churches are multi-ethnic in their make-up. Hereafter I will use only the term multi-congregational.

The Multi-Congregational Church

Pluralism's meteoric rise in the United States contributes to the need for multi-congregational churches. Many areas of the country, formerly populated by a single people group, now find a diversity of people groups living within the neighborhood. These different groups often use different languages, respond to varying cultures, and view the world through different lenses. Persons do not exist as isolated individuals but rather live in networks of social relationships. These varying social networks, which may be either small or large, contribute to the ethnic diversity of most populations, forming what Donald A. McGavran has called the wonderful mosaic of societies.[1] These networks of social relationship demand strategies that relate to the uniqueness of each group. Edward R. Dayton and David A. Fraser state that "The reality of the diversity of groups is the single most important fact in strategies for evangelism."[2]

The diverse groups may share Western, North American culture with members of the other segments but they share together the definite cultural traits of their own social networks. These groups may be linguistic or national. They may respond to regional or traditional tendencies. They may find a base in educational or occupational factors. The diverse groups bind together through some linguistic, cultural, or regional entity.

A community indicates possible need for a multi-congregation church when the cultural and ethnic diversity reaches the place that no one congregation and no one church approach meets the need of the entire population in the community. A congregation that worships and teaches in Spanish will not meet the needs of the Asian people in the area. The Spanish speaking congregation may fail to meet the needs of the Hispanics who prefer to worship in English but still desire a Hispanic congregation. Afro-American groups may desire their own type of music and worship over a pattern of western, middle-class methods. When the changing community incorporates peoples from various regions and cultures, the possibilities exist that a multi-congregational church might well be the answer to evangelistic and church planting effectiveness in the region!

Multi-congregational churches can exist in two forms. The first model acknowledges the racial, ethnic, and linguistic diversity in the community and celebrates the diversity through a multi-hued constituency. Persons from the different cultural networks bind together in the Spirit of Christ and worship together in ways that maintain their varying backgrounds while satisfying their unique needs. This model has special effectiveness in environments where many families are mixed nationally or ethnically.[3]

Another model for the multi-congregational church that exists within a racially and culturally diverse neighborhood is a congregation that is marked by multiple congregations, sharing one facility, each meeting at a different time.[4] C. Peter Wagner quotes Daniel Sanchez, formerly with the Southern Baptist Home Mission Board, then mission executive with the New York State Baptist Convention, and now Professor of Missions at Southwestern Baptist Theological Seminary, as suggesting the multi-congregational model as a primary way for reaching a community undergoing racial, ethnic, and social transition. Wagner declares his belief that this model holds outstanding promise for applying the sociological, theological, biblical, and ethical principles of pluralism in the typical inner-city situation of present-day America.[5]

Sanchez describes these congregations as resembling a corporation composed of several entities (Anglo and ethnic) in which the autonomy of each congregation is preserved and the resources of the entire group combined to present a strong evangelistic witness in the community.[6] Following this plan, the church would have a coordinating pastor—very often the senior pastor of the Anglo congregation. This coordinating pastor would work with an advisory board and coordinating council made up of representitves from each of the congregations. The church would also be guided by various committees also composed of persons from each of the congregations.[7]

In a multi-congregational church, the Anglo group may be called upon to provide a large portion of the finances. The economic facts may show these members to be better able to give the funds to support the work. In such arrangements, the Anglo congregation should come to see the situation in terms of the "Horbet Burger" principle. This principle comes from the experience of the new restaurant owner who declared he would serve "horbet burgers." Upon being queried about the nature of "horbet burgers" the owner explained this delicacy to be made from 50 percent rabbit and 50 percent horse. "How," asked a critic, "do you get exactly 50 percent horse and 50 percent rabbit?" "Easy," answered the owner, "I use one horse and one rabbit!"

The Anglo congregation may supply a great percentage of the money. The Anglos should, however, accept the arrangement as a 50/50 situation. The blessing of aiding the work of the kingdom and the evangelization of the various groups should be reward enough for the Anglo givers.

Peter Wagner describes the structure of a multi-congregational church, the Temple Baptist Church (American Baptist) of Los Angeles, California. The charter of this church declares that members are accepted as part of the total Church Body and are free to choose, apply to, and work within the congregation of their choice. This project, which began in 1969, had by 1974 attained the level of four semiautonomous congregations with plans for between six and twelve. The first four congregations served Anglo, Korean, Hispanic, and Chinese groups. The Chinese group was subdivided into Mandarin, Cantonese, and Swatow language groups. Thai and Vietnamese groups were beginning to meet in 1976. On the first Sunday of each quarter, all the congregations meet together for what is called the "Sounds of Heaven" celebration. These joint services include the Lord's Supper, testimonies, songs (but no sermons) all in the individual languages. Often Christian songs are sung with the same lyrics but in the individual languages. Wagner states, "Here is an example of preserving homogeneity in the fellowship spheres, while introducing creative relationships of love through acquaintance in the heterogeneous intercongregational sphere."[8]

Russell Chandler points to the St. John the Baptist Roman Catholic Church in Baldwin Park, California. The Spanish service for the Latino crowd (the largest of the meetings) is held on Saturday evenings. Cambodian, Laotian, and Vietnamese congregations meet on Sunday mornings. A Cantonese service is held on Sunday evenings. Ministries to Filipinos are featured. The English service, the smallest of the congregations, meets on Sunday afternoon. While most of the attenders at the English service are Anglos, several Afro-Americans and Orientals also attend.

The pastoral staff is cosmopolitan—with the senior pastor a French Canadian, who speaks Spanish, an associate pastor who is Filipino, and another associate pastor Salvadoran. An Italian priest who is learning to speak English joined the staff in 1989, while the seminary intern was Irish-German. Services are given in various languages and sermons often repeated in various tongues.[9]

Daniel Sanchez offers the example of the Nineteenth Avenue Baptist Church of San Francisco which combines four congregations—Anglo, Chinese, Japanese, and Estonian. In the first ten years of this arrangement, some Anglos left the church but the Anglo congregation still doubled and their financial offerings tripled. New members are free to join any congregation and some Japanese and Chinese have chosen to attend the English service. Others, however, prefer to worship in their native tongues. Once a month, the four congregations meet jointly for the Lord's Supper with all four pastors leading. Sanchez declares that these diverse groups are working harmoniously.[10]

Ralph H. Elliott relates his experience with the North Shore Baptist Church in the Uptown-Edgewater section of Chicago. The Church is now made up of congregations serving Chinese, Japanese, and Hispanic groups. Elliott hastens to explain that these groups are not "churches" using North Shore's building but all are members of North Shore Baptist Church. Except in cases of joint celebration, the worship for the various congregations remains separate, in different parts of the building and in appropriate languages. Elliott explains that the diversity in the neighborhood demands this diversity in the church.[11]

The multi-congregational church does provide a viable model for many of the culturally diverse regions of the United States and other countries. Once the multi-congregational church begins to function, it must find ways to continue it's development. Some methods will be the same as used by other, mono-congregational churches. Other means will be distinctive to multi-congregational churches. The remainder of this chapter seeks ways that multi-congregational churches can prepare for revivals.

Preparing Multi-Congregational Churches for Revival Meetings

Like in other churches, revival most often comes to multi-congregational churches when the church members prepare for the revival meetings and seek the power of the Holy Spirit. Fasting, prayer, Bible study, renewal of Christian behavior, increased attention to the unchurched remain as necessary for a multi-congregational church as for any other religious body. These necessary preparations for a revival meeting must never be neglected but rather intensified by multi-congregational churches.

Due to their special natures, multi-congregational churches have unique needs and some of these needs relate to revival meeting preparation. I will set out some attitudes and convictions that the multi-congregational church must seek and some direct methods of preparing for revival.

Revival meeting preparation in a multi-congregational church requires in a special way a Kingdom perspective. Each congregation must be concerned about the people in the other social groups. All spirit of mine must decline and feelings of ours intensify. There should be no "turf-guarding" that would cause one segment of the congregation to exalt its needs over those of some other group. Of greatest importance to each congregation is the increase of the Kingdom of God not the advance of the particular group. The multi-congregational church in a revival meeting seeks kingdom growth rather than church growth.

Revival meeting preparation in a multi-congregational church requires in a special way a unity among segments. Unity holds a unique place in revival in every church but the multi-congregational fellowship must pay even more attention to unity. If one segment of the church plans a revival meeting, every segment should join in the prayer and other preparation for the event. Members of the Hispanic congregation might even join in the visitation for the Asian segment. The entire church should consider itself in the revival meeting when any segment seeks such refreshing and outreach.

The unity within the multi-congregational church can be enhanced during times of revival meeting. The segments can meet together for prayer and preparation. One group can reinforce the efforts of another group. Unity in the Lord and his work overshadows the diversity in cultural and social factors. The senior pastor can visit and encourage the segment preparing for the revival meeting. The entire pastoral staff can participate in the revival meeting preparation and effort in any one segment. Unity undergirds revival preparation in all churches but especially in multi-congregational churches.

Revival meeting preparation in a multi-congregational church requires in a special way intensive marketing. The segment of the church that seeks revival reaches out to a specific target group—i.e. Filipinos in San Francisco, Indonesians in Dallas, Hispanics in Detroit. Persons from regional and linguistic areas will often travel long distances to attend church in their national languages and ways. This fact demands that information (advertisement) of the revival meeting be widely circulated so as to catch the attention of all the peoples from the particular group. Good marketing techniques enhance revival meeting preparation in multi-congregational churches.

Revival meeting preparation in a multi-congregational church requires in a special way the formation of up-to-date and comprehensive prospect lists. The formation of these lists can be seen as part of the marketing techniques mentioned above. In the multi-congregational church, a search should be made to reach out to every member of the target group. Using telephone books, cultural clubs and groups, and personal acquaintances, the congregation seeking revival will develop this comprehensive prospect list. The segment seeking revival will then reach out to seek support from the rest of the church.

Revival meeting preparation in a multi-congregational church requires in a special way attention to social and community needs within the target population. Often the doors to soul-winning are opened by meeting social needs within the families of the social network. These needs can vary from requirements for food, shelter, clothing, or other physical necessities to help with job training, placement, or legal advisement. This social and community involvement should, of course, be an ongoing, never-ending ministry. The involvement may well be intensified as the revival meeting approaches. Here again, the possibility of interaction and mutual helpfulness can be reached by inter-congregational service.

Revival meeting preparation in a multi-congregational church might in a special way use the methodology of simultaneous revival meetings. The different congregations could plan together for a revival meeting at the same time or closely related times. In this plan, preparation could be carried out together. Marketing expenses and efforts could be shared. Mutual concern and service could be enhanced. Associations and other groupings of church have long used simultaneous revival meeting methods to great effectiveness. The method could well enhance the overall ministry of the multi-congregational church.

Conclusion

In the constantly changing scene in most parts of the world today, more and more social networks of peoples find themselves living in proximity to other groups of peoples. Experience has taught that target group congregations enhance evangelism. Often, in areas where ethnic and other people groups live, one finds too few people to plant a strong church in any one linguistic or social group. In such cases, a multi-congregational church may best meet the needs.

Like all other churches, the multi-congregational church stands in need of periodic revival and evangelistic emphases. This chapter sets out a few guidelines for multi-congregational churches as they strive to experience revival and increase evangelistic effectiveness.

Endnotes

1. Donald A. McGavran, *Understanding Church Growth*, rev. ed. (Grand Rapids: Eerdmans, 1990), 43ff.

2. *Planning Strategies for World Evangelism*, Rev. (Grand Rapids: Eerdmans (MARC), 1990), 82.

3. Russell Chandler, *Racing Toward 2001* (Grand Rapids: Zondervan Publishing, 1992, 32).

4. Thom S. Rainer, *The Book of Church Growth* (Nashville: Broadman Press, 1993, 212.

5. C. Peter Wagner, *Our Kind of People* (Atlanta: John Knox Press, 1979), 159.

6. Daniel Sanchez, "Viable Models for Churches in Communities Experiencing Ethnic Transition," unpublished paper, Fuller Theological Seminary, 1976.

7. Wagner, *Our Kind of People*, 161.

8. Wagner, *Our Kind of People*, 160.

9. Chandler, *Racing Toward 2001*, 32-33, 264-70.

10. Sanchez, "Viable Models."

11. Ralph H. Elliott, *Church Growth that Counts* (Valley Forge: Judson Press, 1982), 11-12.

Ebbie C. Smith is Professor of Christian Ethics and Missions at Southwestern Baptist Theological Seminary, Fort Worth, Texas and occupant of the John and Vida Cooper Chair of Missions.

Preparing for a Revival Meeting in an Hispanic Church

There is a sense in which revival meetings in an Hispanic church are not too different from those which take place in English speaking churches. These usually involve praying, inviting people, singing, preaching, giving an invitation, and discipling the converts. But there is also a sense in which revival meetings in an Hispanic church have some distinctive characteristics which need to be taken into account in the planning process. We will consider some of these as we focus on three major components of revival meetings: the prospect, the preparation, and the proclamation.

The Prospect

Most Hispanics do not have an evangelical background. This means that we cannot take it for granted that they will understand the plan of salvation the first time (or times) they hear it, nor that they will have a positive attitude toward the idea of attending a revival meeting in an evangelical church. Because of their religious tradition, they often have an inclination to rely on the religious rituals of their church versus having a personal experience of salvation in

Jesus Christ. In addition to this, some of them have grown up with an ingrained suspicion of evangelical Christians ("Protestants"), and at times feel strong pressures from their families and friends to remain within their religious tradition. This means, therefore, that for many Hispanics a decision to receive Christ and to follow Him in active discipleship within the fellowship of an evangelical church has both *spiritual* and *social* dimensions.[1]

For many Hispanics, coming to a personal experience of salvation in Jesus Christ is the result of a process. In his book *Contemporary Christian Communication*,[2] James Engel describes a sort of pilgrimage (or count down) as a person comes to the point of deciding to commit his or her life to Christ. Engel's scale begins with persons who have a vague awareness of a supreme being and traces them to the point where they make a decision to receive Christ.

The pilgrimage of most Hispanics who have come to a personal experience of salvation in Jesus Christ has been somewhat different from that which Engel describes. Their experience can be described more accurately in the following manner:

- 8 Knowledge that the one true God exists
- 7 Knowledge that Jesus Christ is the Son of God
- 6 Knowledge that Jesus died on the cross
- 5 Realization that Jesus died on the cross for *me*
- 4 Realization that *I* need to receive Jesus' saving grace
- 3 Realization that this saving grace comes through a *personal experience with Jesus* (not through religious rituals)
- 2 Decision to act despite social pressures
- 1 Repentance and personal faith in Jesus as Savior and Lord

As can be seen in the above scale, Hispanics generally have more than a vague knowledge of a supreme being. They know that the one true God exists. They do not need to be convinced that Jesus died on the cross. They focus on this every Lenten season. What they often fail to realize, however, is that Jesus died for *them* and that they need to make a *personal decision* to accept Jesus Christ in order to receive His saving grace, rather than receiving this grace through religious rituals.

But this decision does not take place in a vacuum. Often when Hispanics make a decision to receive Christ and to following Him in discipleship in the fellowship of an evangelical church, they experience severe social pressures. This means, therefore, that the cultivation of a relationship is often indispensable in order to lead Hispanics to a personal faith in Christ. In other words, whereas in many Anglo churches people are *won* to the Lord and then *incorporated* into the fellowship of the church, in Hispanic churches often people need to be *incorporated* into the fellowship of the family of the church and then *won* to the Lord.

The Preparation

The fact that most Hispanics do not have an evangelical background has significant implications for our personal and public evangelistic efforts.

A. Implications for Personal Evangelism

As we have seen in the modified Engel scale, many persons know some of the facts that relate to the death of Jesus on the cross but they have not made a personal application of these facts to their lives. In other words, they have not had a personal experience of salvation in Jesus Christ.

In order for Hispanics to come to the point of repentance and conversion, it is often necessary for them to develop a personal relationship with someone who is an evangelical Christian. This means, therefore that relational (friendship) evangelism is often the most effective approach to lead Hispanics to Christ.

In making preparation for a revival, it is very helpful if church members can be encouraged to begin to cultivate friendships with non-believers months before the meeting itself. This means that church members need to spend time with the prospects by: (1) inviting them to their homes for a meal; (2) ministering to them when they have needs; (3) remembering them during special occasions (holidays, birthdays); (4) inviting them to special events (e.g. sports events, movie, concert, drama); and (5) simply being a sympathetic, caring friend in times of celebration, of sorrow, and of transition.

This type of Christian friendship lays a foundation for a gospel witness to be given. When a genuine friendship has been established the witness is often much more sensitive to the way in which the gospel needs to be presented to that particular person. As a result of this friendship, the prospect is often much more receptive to the presentation of the gospel. Relational evangelism, therefore, is often a prerequisite for a truly effective revival meeting in an Hispanic church.

B. Implications for Public Evangelism

Just as it is important to establish personal relationships with prospects, it is necessary to have cultivative events prior to a revival meeting.

In addition to having a very limited knowledge of the Gospel, many Hispanics, because of their religious tradition, have a sense of fear or suspicion with regard to evangelical Christians.

This means that the vast majority of Hispanics will not attend an Evangelical Church the first time they are invited. Often they need to be invited to cultivative events in preparation for the time when the revival is going to be held. These events include such activities as: (1) Home Bible Studies; (2) Dramas (Easter, Christmas, pageants); (3) Musicals; (4) ministries to the community, and (5) church sponsored recreational activities. Often these activities become a bridge between Hispanic prospects and the church. As they participate in these cultivative activities, they begin to realize that there are many good and helpful things which take place in an evangelical Hispanic church. Again, we make the very important point that Hispanic prospects must first become a part of the fellowship of a church before they believe in Jesus Christ as their personal Savior.

Cultivation, therefore, is indispensable in both personal and public evangelism. In planning for a revival meeting, it is very helpful to *train* and *involve* church members in cultivative activities. This will ensure that when the time for the revival comes, there will be Hispanic prospects in attendance who have already overcome some of the obstacles of limited knowledge of the Gospel and apprehension regarding evangelical worship services.

The Proclamation

When Hispanic prospects attend a revival meeting, they need to find an environment which facilitates their response to the Gospel. The worship service, therefore, is very important. As the revival service is being planned, it is important to view everything from the perspective of the prospect. This includes the music, recognition of visitors, announcements, offering, preaching and invitation.

A. The Music

Music plays a vital role in a revival meeting. It either sets a worshipful, positive, joyful tone or it becomes a negative factor which dampens the Spirit and distracts the people. As is true of other churches, the selection of music for a revival meeting in an Hispanic church requires much prayer, thought, and planning. Planning the music from the perspective of the prospect, however, requires additional attention.

First, because of the fact that many Hispanic prospects are not accustomed to singing from a hymn book, it is helpful to print the hymns and choruses in the bulletin. In addition to this, the songs which are selected should be simple and understandable. That is to say, these songs should not contain difficult theological terms which only insiders can understand.

Second, because Hispanic prospects are not used to singing very much, the number of congregational songs, which are sung should be limited to a few. In their place, there should be a greater emphasis on special music. Even if a church does not have a choir, it can use a praise group, duets, quartets, and solos to enhance the music which is used in a revival meeting.

Third, the style of music and the instruments which are used should reflect the culture of the Hispanic church. In selecting these, a distinction should be made between the *form* and the *meaning*. The meaning of the songs should be thoroughly biblical but there can be flexibility in the style of the music. In most instances, the extent to which the music reflects the culture of the congregation, has a direct bearing on the way in which it touches the heart of the people.

B. The Recognition of Visitors

Many Hispanic church members believe that the best way to welcome visitors is to get them to stand up, tell their name, and be seen by everybody. While it is true that church members generally enjoy being recognized in that manner when they visit other churches, the truth is that Hispanic visitors are often terrified when they are asked to stand and speak before the group.

Two of the main reasons why visitors are recognized in that manner is that: (1) we want to make them feel welcome and (2) we want to have a record of their visit so that we can contact them later. These two important goals can be accomplished in other ways. First, people can be made to feel welcome by getting everyone to stand and greet one another while a song of welcome is being sung. Second, the names and addresses of the visitors can be obtained by having cards in the pews to be filled out and deposited in the offering plate. Other ways of doing this is by asking the church members who invited them to fill out cards or by having greeters at the door handing out the visitor's cards. Visitors can be welcomed without becoming the object of attention.

C. Announcements

The vast majority of the announcements have very little meaning to the visitors. When a great deal of time is spent making "insider" announcements, the spirit of worship is interrupted and the outsiders feel either confused or excluded. Two things can be helpful at this point: (1) printed them in the bulletin so that church members can read them, and (2) make announcements which are of general interest after the invitation. This will prevent interruptions and enable church members to remember them.

D. The Offering

Offerings are often very important in revival meetings. Many times, especially in smaller churches, offerings are needed to defray the expenses of the revival meeting (e.g., honorarium, travel expenses, and lodging for the evangelistic team). There is one problem, Hispanic visitors in many instances come from a religious tradition that does not emphasize tithing and sacrificial giving.

Several things can be done to defray the expenses of the revival meeting while at the same time avoiding offending the visitors. First, the church can budget these expenses in advance. Second, the church can give out love offering envelopes prior to the revival meeting. Third, the offering can be taken up at the end of the service after the invitation. Fourth, and more importantly, when the offering is taken up the minister can explain that the visitors are not being asked to give. Some pastors explain: "We invite the members to participate in this offering. Those of you who are visiting, please don't feel obligated, we would be happy to get your visitor's card." It is important to communicate to visitors that we are interested in their spiritual welfare, not their money.

E. The Evangelistic Sermon

Undoubtedly the most important aspect of the revival service is the proclamation of the Gospel. While it is true that the Gospel is communicated through the songs and the fellowship, it is also true that the evangelistic sermon is the focal point of the proclamation of Gospel. In order to be effective in this awesome responsibility, it is important to keep several things in mind pertaining to the background of the Hispanic visitors.

First, the evangelistic sermon in an Hispanic congregation should focus on the biblical message. Practices such as criticizing the religious tradition of Hispanics who are not evangelical or emphasizing why the Evangelical church is right, offend visitors and detract from the proclamation of the Gospel. As the apostle Paul, we must "preach Christ."

Second, the evangelistic sermon in an Hispanic congregation should not take it for granted that the visitors have a knowledge of the Bible which enables them to understand references to biblical characters, events, and texts. The sermon, therefore, should be explained in simple terms. A brief background to other portions of Scripture should be provided so that visitors can get the full meaning of the message.

Third, the evangelistic sermon in an Hispanic church should not be highly theoretical in its content. Due to the fact that the majority of the visitors do not have a theological background, it is better to select the portions of Scripture which lend themselves for the communication of the Gospel. A series of sermons, for example, on the parables of Jesus (such as the Prodigal Son, the Lost Sheep, and the Rich Man and Lazarus) can help people to visualize in their minds the teachings of Christ regarding salvation. Another approach can be a series of sermons on the people (such persons as Nicodemus, the Samaritan Woman, Zachaeus, Peter, John and Matthew) who had a life-changing encounter with Jesus Christ. These sermons can focus on what the life of these individuals was before they met Christ, how they came to know Christ, and the difference that this encounter made in their lives. One of the strengths of this approach is that it focuses on the need to have a personal experience of salvation with Jesus Christ. This series of sermons, therefore, can help non-evangelical Hispanics to understand that they must experience the new birth (c.f., John 3) by means of a personal commitment to faith in Jesus Christ. Yet another series of evangelistic sermons which can help the Hispanic visitors to understand the Gospel is one which focuses on key events in the life of Christ. Events such as the birth, the death, the resurrection and the ascension can establish bridges between what they know about the Bible and what they need to know about salvation. The description of these events can help the hearers to form mental images which will communicate more clearly and forcefully the basic truth about the Gospel.

Fourth, the evangelistic sermon in an Hispanic church should be felt as well as understood. Members as well as visitors in Hispanic churches respond better if the sermons touch their emotions as well as their intellect. The evangelist, therefore, should not be afraid to show some emotion while he is preaching. Conveying joy, sorrow, compassion and other emotions through the words that are utilized, facial expression, and tone of voice can help the listener to feel the thoughts that are being expressed. The use of carefully selected illustrations can also help the listeners to comprehend and internalize the Gospel message. One of the reasons why Jesus was so effective in communicating the Gospel message was that he used illustration (parables) and expressions from the common life of the people.

Evangelistic sermons in Hispanic churches, therefore, should focus on the gospel message, should be explained in simple terms, should have a balance between the theoretical and the practical, and should be felt as well as understood.

F. The Evangelistic Invitation

Due to the fact that many of the visitors in an Hispanic church do not have an evangelical background, there are some things that need to be considered while giving the invitation.

First, one should not take it for granted that a person who comes to the front at the time of the invitation fully understands the meaning of this action. At times people who come forward simply want someone to pray for a need that they have. At other times the persons have felt an emotion but they have not really thought through the implications of that decision. Two things can help to minimize confusion at this point. One is to ask the person, "what is the desire of your heart?" This keeps us from putting words in the mouths of the people. For example, if you ask, "you have come forward to receive Christ, right?" They are going to say "yes." But that does not necessarily mean that that is the decision they are making. The other way to avoid confusion is to have some trained counselors who will take them to a room, read the plan of salvation to them, and then involve them in a prayer of repentance and acceptance of Christ.

Second, because of their religious background, many times visitors feel touched by the sermon but they are afraid to come to the front. Several approaches can help to deal with this timidity. One approach is to take them through some steps gradually. First, you can ask all of the people in the congregation to bow their heads, close their eyes, and pray. Second, you can ask those who want to receive Christ to repeat a simple prayer with you. Third, you can ask those who have prayed the prayer to raise their hands so that you can have the privilege of praying for them. Fourth, you can ask those who raised their hands to come forward while the invitation song is being sung. At this point it is important to keep three things in mind. One is that you need to explain to people what is going to happen when they come forward. Many do not have an idea as to what you are going to do. It is helpful, therefore for you to tell them, "I am going to ask you to come to the front where I will have a brief word of prayer with you and then you will go to the counseling room where one of our trained counselors is going to share some printed materials with you that will help you to understand your decision better and to know how to continue to grow in your walk with God." Another important thing is that you need to come down from the platform and be at the front to receive those who are making decisions, pray with them, and direct them to the counselors. Finally you need to leave the door open for those who raised their hands but did not come forward. You may say something like this, "let me just say to those of you who raised your hands but did not come forward, I know how difficult it is to come forward in front of so many people. I appreciate the fact that you indicated a desire to know more about Jesus Christ. Let me encourage you to talk with me, with the pastor, or with the person who invited you to the service tonight. We want to answer your questions and to help you to respond to the voice of God which you felt in your heart tonight."

Third, it may be extremely difficult for some Hispanic visitors to raise their hands and come to the front. You may simply want to ask all of the people in the congregation to bow their heads in prayer. You may then ask the people who want to receive Christ to look up and direct their attention to you while everyone else is praying. As they look at you, you may want to explain briefly the importance of their decision to receive Christ. You may then ask them to repeat the sinner's prayer with you and then fill out a card which has been placed in the pew rack in front of them, indicating the decision they are making, and including their name and telephone number so that you can visit them in their home, answer their questions, and pray with them.

Generally, Hispanic visitors do not make a decision as readily as those who have an evangelical background. However, with much prayer and patience, you can be led by the Lord to utilize the invitation method which is most suitable for that congregation.

Conclusion

While Hispanic and Anglo churches have many things in common, there are some key factors which need to be kept in mind in planning and conducting a revival meeting in an Hispanic church. Because most of the Hispanics do not have an evangelical background, much cultivation will be needed in both personal and public evangelistic activities. The music which is sung needs to be selected with the knowledge that most visitors are not accustomed to singing congregational songs, do not understand some of our religious vocabulary, and respond better if the music reflects their culture. Visitors should be welcomed in general terms but not pointed out or asked to speak. Announcements should be kept to a minimum and preferably given at the end of the service. Visitors should be told that it is the member's responsibility and not theirs to participate in the offering unless they feel led of the Lord to do so. The evangelistic sermons should be biblical, simple, practical, and heart-felt. The invitation should clarify what people are being asked to do, involve the use of counselors and provide options so that those who are timid and have questions will be followed up as well as those who have made their decision public. Finally, all efforts pertaining to a revival meeting in an Hispanic church should be saturated with prayer. "If the Lord does not build the house, those who labor, labor in vain."

End Notes

1. Hesselgrave points this out when he describes the process as (1) discovery, (2) deliberation, and (3) determination. However, that is not the end of the process. Often people face (4) dissonance, and may either experience (5) reversion (due to social pressures), or (5) discipline. David J. Hesselgrave, *Communicating Christ Cross-culturally*, pp. 447-457.

2. See James F. Engel, *Contemporary Christian Communication* (New York: Thomas Nelson Publishers, 1976), p. 81.

Daniel R. Sanchez is the Vernon and Jeanette Davidson Professor of Missions and Director of the Scarborough Institute at Southwestern Baptist Theological Seminary in Fort Worth, Texas.

Preparing for a Revival Meeting in a Black Church

First, let us establish the fact that there is only one Church.[1] To refer to it as black or white is to admit that we have failed to uphold Christ's true purpose for His Church.[2] However, addressing the task before me, "Preparing for a Revival Meeting in a Black Church," I will be the first to admit that present within black culture are certain distinctives which rise from a history of experiences that has shaped who we are as a people. Christianity in the black tradition evolved from an African culture which was not unlike the culture from which primitive Christianity arose.[3] It is from this background that a unique approach to the worship of God can be recognized. And revival is no exception.

The major difference between the church in the African American community and others lies in the reality that since its inception it has been the backbone and nucleus for all activity and advancement among its people. The church ". . . served to alleviate many of the frustrations, anxieties, and fears emanating from economic exploitation and sociopolitical repression that blacks experienced under the castelike structure of the South.[4] Therefore, the need for revival is perceived differently in the African American community. Revival is expected to bring strengthening for survival and incentive for service. Thus, "it must always speak to the condition within our existence."[5] The story is told of one black preacher who, after receiving the news that his church building had just burned down, gathered the congregation together and said, "Babies, we gonna have revival!" This type of attitude is exemplary of a shift in the African American community in which ". . . the revival no longer causes large numbers of conversions,"[6] but is now a vehicle used to rekindle the spirits of church members.

One can readily perceive that the motivation and expectation for revival in the African American community is quite different. These differences require a preacher/evangelist who possesses a keen awareness of the condition of African Americans and a willingness to be guided by the Holy spirit as he prepares for the revival meeting.

Let me set your mind at ease as preparation for a revival meeting begins. You in no way can bring revival to any group of people at any time or in any place. To even think that you can in some way bring about revival is to completely misunderstand the nature and source of revival. The responsibility of the preacher is not to bring about repentance and revival, but to bring the Word of God, which has the power to give life to the dead, dull, and dispirited.

In the little book by Strack and Witty, *The New Testament Way to Revival*, a four-fold formula for revival is presented: prayer, publicity, preaching, and priority.[7] Of these four components, prayer and preaching are of particular importance as one prepares to lead a revival meeting. These two requirements are basic and apply whether revival takes place in an African American context or not.

Prayer

The absolute most important ingredient in preparing for a revival meeting is prayer. Nothing can short circuit true revival more than prayerlessness. As a boy growing up in church I often heard my pastor say, "little prayer, little power; much prayer, much power!" Although I'm sure the phrase didn't begin with him, the truth of it is nevertheless effectual. There is no earthly substitute for prayer![8] Since revival is sent from heaven, "there is little else, besides praying, men can do to bring revival."[9]

As you begin to seek guidance from the Holy Spirit in the weeks that lead up to the actual revival meeting, many benefits can be gained from choosing a like-minded person as a partner in prayer. However, nothing can take the place of the preacher's own personal one-on-one time with God. The time you spend in your own secret closet wrestling with God in prayer will produce spiritual fruit for yourself and those who hear you. The statement is true that "no man is greater than his prayer life."[10]

If revival is going to take place in the hearts of the preacher and the people, it must first begin with an extraordinary spirit of prayer.[11] After personal soul searching and prayer for cleansing and revival you are ready to extend your prayers to the church with whom you will be sharing the Word of God.

First of all, prayers should be made for the pastor of the church where the revival meeting will take place. In a limited sense he holds the key to the success of the upcoming week of services. Let me explain. The role the pastor plays is prepollant because he remains in contact with his members and the evangelist. His insight with regards to the spiritual condition of the church should be of immense value as messages are being prepared for that week. His role is crucial also because he will be responsible for leading the church in prayer in the weeks prior to the revival meeting. Owens sees the pastor's role as most crucial when he says, "Failure to give godly leadership in seeking times of unusual spiritual awakening could be the most serious flaw in any pastor's entire ministry.[12]

Secondly, consistent prayers should be lifted in behalf of the congregation. The revival meeting in the black tradition of worship has become a time of celebration and a relieving of burdens.[13] While these are pertinent reasons for anticipating a revival meeting, they cannot stand in lieu of true repentance and the desire to win souls for the kingdom of God. The preparedness of the congregation is crucial to the success of any revival meeting. If the people have not reached the point or recognizing their own need for repentance and renewal, revival cannot take place. Because the congregation stands to benefit the most from the revival meeting, their hearts and minds must be open to receive all that the Spirit is willing to pour out to them. Pray that all hindrances would be removed in order that the Lord may have absolute control in their lives.[14]

Finally, in some cases, your preaching assignment will involve small town churches or isolated communities. Prayers offered should include those who are not directly connected with your church. All trepidation at this point should desist. Don't be afraid to ask God for an extraordinary out pouring of His Spirit during the weeks of revival meetings and then be prepared for an abundant harvest.

Preaching

No one can deny that revival is always preceded by fervent and earnest prayer. Revivals are prayed down! Yet, revival is never genuine revival without an emphasis on the Word of God. Whether it is the conversion of the lost, the restoration of the backslidden, or the encouragement of the mature, God's means of accomplishing this is through His preached Word. Although other aspects of worship enhance the total experience, "the sermon is the heart of the worship experience[15] and cannot be substituted!

Today, there has been a tendency to make all components of worship equivalent. However, in the black experience of worship, the sermon remains at the center. This fact necessitates a preacher who has spent the proper amount of time in preparing himself for the preaching event. As stated earlier, that preparation begins with the preacher's personal repentance and soul cleansing. There is much to be said about the spiritual condition of the one who would be used of God as an instrument of revival. Suffice it to say, "the greatest quality in good preaching is the holy character of the man who preaches."[16] Unless he is full of God and the Bible, he cannot interpret either rightly.[17]

Up to now you will recognize that the basic requirements for revival are essentially the same. At what point then is there a noticeable difference in how one prepares for revival meeting in the African-American community? The answer is obviously in the preaching. This chapter is included in this present work, not because black preaching is aberrant, but because it is a unique and desirable form of divine communication that stirs the souls of those who hear it. The fascination of others with regard to black preaching can be traced back to "a certain openness and permissiveness that makes it possible for a person to do almost anything he wants to if he does it sincerely."[18] This frees the preacher to be himself and not feel restrained by the requirements and expectations of any group of people.

Hamilton and Ellison regard the black evangelist as "a man of extravagant gifts and unrestrained emotions who speaks fluently and loudly . . ."[19] Don't suppose that a black congregation is looking for an evangelist who has to prove through his language and mannerisms that he is erudite. A revival meeting is not the time to impress the church with your "much learning." Allow the Holy Spirit to get maximum use out of your own character and personality.

The majority of time spent in preparation must be reserved for developing the sermons that will be preached during the revival meeting. This responsibility means merging good, authentic, homiletic form into a powerful, soul-stirring message. At one time Black people usually judged a message by its ability to incite some kind of emotional experience which allowed them to release the frustrations and burdens of an oppressive existence. Mitchell is correct in pointing out that for the most part, black preaching has historically focused upon the daily struggles of the people.[20] Although much of the emotionalism which is characteristic of our people remains, most desire to be spiritually stretched and nourished by the preached Word.

Therefore, your task is to prepare the holistic message; one which touches the heart and at the same time stimulates the thought processes. For far too long churches in the African-American community have settled for sermons that reach the emotive realms of the mind to the neglect of the intellectual. In addition to the word which calms fears and eases burdens, must come the challenge and call to a life that draws each one to a closer walk with the Lord Jesus. However, a word of warning. Avoid the temptations to impress the hearers with your exegetical excellence and hot-shot hermeneutics. This type of "head to head" preaching[21] does wonders for the mind, but usually leaves the soul wanting. Save the sermon on supralapsarianism for preaching lab.

The inexperienced preacher who comes from the black tradition of worship stands at all times in a most precarious position. On the one hand, he must be true to his culture and the rich heritage of black preaching which preceded him. On the other hand, he must not allow his culture to suppress his new found dianoetic virtues, which both enhance and advance black preaching as a whole. This means the inexperienced preacher must be a bridge between two cultures. He must prove to the church in the African-American community that advanced learning is not designed to hinder spirituality but rather to enhance it.

He must be able to reach the souls of black folk with Soul language, putting them at ease and gaining maximum access by avoiding all the linguistic signals of social distance from his congregation. Yet he must be able to reinforce and keep alive the language learnings of the young people of his congregation which link them to the larger community.[22]

Recently, I had the opportunity to go home and was given the privilege to preach to the church where I grew up. After preaching what would be considered by seminary standards, a doctrinal sermon, the congregation was lifted to a celebration of joy and new hope. Immediately following the celebration the pastor commented that I had preached a real good message and that it wasn't a "seminary message" but was indeed the gospel of Jesus Christ!

If the evangelist is going to be effective in the African-American community he must develop the ability to communicate "bilingually."[23] The task of preparing for a revival meeting within any culture is a sober undertaking. The one who would lead a revival meeting in the African-American community must first pay close attention to his own spiritual condition and remember to preach in the language of the people.

Endnotes

1. Ephesians 4:4-6.

2. Colossians 3:9-11.

3. Henry Mitchell, "Black Preaching," *Black Church Lifestyles*, ed. Emmanuel L. McCall (Nashville: Broadman Press, 1986), 110.

4. Hans A. Baer and Merrill Singer, *African-American Religion in the Twentieth Century: Varieties of Protest and Accommodation* (Knoxville: University of Tennessee Press, 1992), 39.

5. Rev. Isadore Edwards, Jr. Interview by author, tape recording, Ft. Worth, TX, June 2, 1995.

6. Benjamin Elijah Mays and Joseph Williams, *The Negroes Church* (New York: Arno Press, 1969), 253.

7. Jay Strack and Robert G. Witty, *The New Testament Way to Revival* (Nashville: Broadman Press, 1989), 22.

8. James 5:16.

9. Richard Owen Roberts, *Revival* (Illinois: Richard Owen Roberts Publishers, 1982), 122.

10. Leonard Ravenhill, *Why Revival Tarries* (Minneapolis: Bethany House Publishers), 23.

11. Roberts, 58.

12. Ibid., 107.

13. Dr. Asa W. Sampson, interview by author, tape recording, Ft. Worth, TX, July 13, 1995.

14. Roberts, 115-20.

15. James H. Harris, *Pastoral Theology: A Black Church Perspective* (Minneapolis: Fortress Press, 1991), 98.

16. Jonas Oramel Peck, *The Revival and the Pastor* (New York: Eaton and Mains, 1894), 116.

17. Ibid.

18. Mitchell, *Black Church Lifestyles*, 120.

19. Baer and Singer, 35.

20. Mitchell, *Black Church Lifestyles*, 101.

21. Roberts, 17.

22. Henry Mitchell, *Black Preaching* (New York: J. B. Lippincott, 1970), 152.

23. Ibid., 153.

Raymond Spencer is a Ph.D. Student in Preaching at Southwestern Baptist Theological Seminary in Fort Worth, Texas and serves as Assistant to the Pastor at New Rising Star Baptist Church in Fort Worth.

Preparing to Minister
To and With the Pastor

Did you hear about the pastor who went to the air terminal to pick up the guest evangelist? He spotted him coming down the escalator with a golf bag over one shoulder and a tennis racket under his arm. His first words were: "Hello, pastor! Could you carry these clubs for me, and by the way, can you loan me a New Testament for the week?"

An exaggeration, of course, but there have been instances in which a preacher arrived at a church without a clear view of his reason for being there. That reason must be to serve in the name of Christ. One of the best ways of serving is to befriend and encourage the pastor. Ministering to the pastor may be a new idea to you. Likely, concentration has been focused on preparing evangelistic sermons, sharpening witnessing skills, and anticipating everything that will be expected.

The awesome responsibility of leading evangelistic services at the request of a church produces mixed feelings. You have dreamed of "doing revivals" but a feeling of inadequacy surfaces. Possibly, the sermons you will preach are the first *evangelistic* sermons you have prepared. You may not have worked closely with a pastor before. Your relational skills may have been tested only in familiar surroundings. Your knowledge of the church and the pastor is limited. You are excited about the opportunity but are questioning what you have to offer. With fear and trembling you wonder why you ever accepted such a responsibility!

What You Have to Offer

What do you have to offer that can bless the pastor? He probably has more experience in ministry; he may be older. What do you have that will benefit him? You have much to share that God can utilize to minister to the pastor.

You have *yourself.* Neither your salvation nor your call was an accident. God saved you on purpose for a purpose. He qualifies and equips those he calls. You are especially equipped by your family, education and experience. God does not waste any of your life experiences, but utilizes everything that makes you who you are.

Trying to be someone else or parroting others' ideas negates why God singled you out to be his servant. His desire is to glorify his name through *your* life. The pastor will be blessed as he sees the result of God's working in your life.

You have your *call.* Church members respect the commitment you have made to vocational Christian service. Your call may be puzzling to many of them. Some have a sense of awe and mystery that God has dealt with you in a way different from them. You may have found it difficult to explain your call to someone else. You may even be mystified that God has called you to vocational ministry. However, you are dedicated to fulfilling this divine call. Sharing this very personal experience with the pastor opens up the possibility of dialogue on a deeper level.

You have your *gospel.* The saving experience in which Christ Jesus became your personal Lord and Savior is good news to be shared. This good news is your gospel. Paul uses the personal pronouns "our" and "my" to show that the gospel belongs to him.[1] The good news penetrated mind and heart until it was, in reality, his gospel.

Your gospel has been entrusted to you to live and declare.[2] This personal gospel motivates and inspires. The pastor will be blessed by witnessing how the gospel has penetrated your heart and mind. It is a spiritual feast when two preachers engage in edifying conversation. To talk about personal experiences and to share how the gospel has become "enfleshed" in you is part of what you have to offer.

During a week of evangelistic services, this is an ongoing conversation. In the car, in the home, and around the dinner table, the "bits and pieces" about each other accumulate into a growing understanding of who we are as God's servants. This exchange is satisfying and enjoyable. Pastors need this kind of fellowship.

Sharing in Ministry

You also will engage in numerous activities during the week of evangelistic services. These include preaching, visiting in businesses and in homes, eating with individuals and groups, and praying. Almost all your time will be spent with the pastor. Sharing this week of ministry together will be a welcome "break" for him from his usual routine.

During this time, a particular way you will minister to the pastor is *by receiving ministry from him.* As a young man I learned much from pastors with whom I served. While still a seminary student I preached in revival services where a fellow student was pastor. He taught me by his example how to witness, even though I was the evangelist!

You may also learn how not to serve. I once worked with a pastor who
had "retired" spiritually, mentally and physically. He only talked about how great the "old days" were. He did not visit; he described any prospects as a "few old soreheads" who didn't want any more visits. He was only going through the motions of pastoral activity. He did what had to be done to hold on to a job. No one desires to end up that way. No one wants to be "dead" yet living. No one wants circumstances to control them. I *learned* much from this experience.

Such a negative example is not the norm. For the most part, you will be blessed and educated in a positive way by the pastor with whom you serve. You will learn the practical side of being a minister: how to prepare a church for a revival meeting, how to relate to the people who are visited, how to involve church members in prayer and visitation, how to increase member participation so that the church as a whole owns the responsibility for revival meeting activities. These are among the things I learned in working with men of God. My life has been enriched. I received more than I could ever give. I am indebted to the pastors with whom I have served as the "evangelist."

So, "go to school" to the pastor. Listen to him, ask him questions, hear his story. Be blessed by him. Receiving his ministry will also bless him.

You also will minister to the pastor *by affirming him and making yourself available for service.* Affirm the pastor by accepting him for who he is. His priorities may not coincide with yours. He may be overwhelmed by financial or family difficulties. His vision for the church may have dimmed. However, remember that he is the pastor because he answered God's call to be there. You are to be redemptive, not judgmental. Accepting the pastor for who he is is an exercise of grace.

Affirm the pastor by listening. Listen to his story, ask questions about his background, his salvation experience, and his spiritual pilgrimage. Your willingness to listen may be the best therapy for him. Some pastors are loners. They are more apt to share with an outsider than with anyone in their community. All of us appreciate "being listened to."

Affirm the pastor both publicly and privately. He has given his life to serving others for Christ's sake. He has given himself to that church and community. His life of faith, his family life, his discernment of the word, his wisdom, his way of doing ministry, his blessing you by example--these should be affirmed to his face and to others.

Affirm the pastor by sharing resources. Share with him what you are doing in your own personal pilgramage. List the books and articles that have been meaningful to you. Share with him the ideas that have challenged you; discuss the theology that has become incarnate in your life.

Be available for service. You are not there to carry out your agenda. Let the pastor know that you are there to serve. Make no special demands. Be willing to visit, to witness, to speak, to preach, to counsel and to enjoy spending time with him and his family.

Pay attention to the pastor's family. Take an interest in each of the children; call them by name; spend time with them, if possible. You may be God's way of encouraging them in their faith.

Treat the pastor's wife as a fellow minister. She may have insights about the church that will aid you in sermon application and counselling. She *also* may need a listening ear.

You will be an effective witness of the Christian life by being sensitive to hurts and disappointments as well as accomplishments and joys that the pastor and his family share with you.

You will also share in ministry and thus minister to the pastor *by being a person of integrity*. The fact that God wants integrity among his ministers is seen in I Chronicles 29:17, "I know, My God, that You test the heart and are pleased with honest intent. And now I have seen with joy how willingly your people who are here have given to You." Likewise, the apostle Paul speaks to this matter of integrity in II Corinthians 8:21, "For we are taking pains to do what is right, not only in the eyes of the Lord but also in the eyes of men." The following are some suggestions that will help you minister through your integrity:

(1) Say nothing for which you are not willing to accept full responsibility.

(2) Beware of the tendency to always comment on every matter under discussion.

(3) Be as positive in your comments as possible.

(4) Avoid plagiarism in speaking.

(5) Do not assume the attitude of authority in areas where your information, experience, and training are incomplete.

(6) Daily ask the Lord to guide you or restrain you in your comments.

(7) Be above reproach in all your personal actions.

(8) Be an example in speech, dress, habits, and lifestyles. Be an example of gentleness in your reactions to others comments, insults, opposition, and hostilities.

(9) Be discreet in your relation to members of the opposite sex.

(10) Maintain a comparatively simple lifestyle in regard to expenses.

(11) Be accurate in all financial reporting with documentation where possible.

(12) Respect the leadership of the local church.

(13) Keep confidences securely.

(14) Regard your service as primary and renumeration for service as secondary.

You have much to share. God will utilize your personality, training, and experience to glorify His name. The church has already prayed for you. The pastor has led in preparing for your coming. You will be heard and you will be loved. A door of opportunity has been opened to you. God has called you. You have a gospel both to live by and to declare. Include ministry to the pastor in the definition of your task as an evangelist.

Endnotes

1. "For we know, brother loved by God, that he has chosen you, because *our* gospel came to you not simply with words, but also with power, with the Holy Spirit and with deep conviction" 1 Thess. 1:4-5a; 2 Tim. 2:8 states "Remember Jesus Christ, raised from the dead, descended from David. This is *my* gospel . . . " (cf. Rom. 2:15; 16:25; 2 Cor. 4:3; 2 Thess. 2:14)

2. cf. 1 Thess. 2:4; 1 Tim. 1:11; Gal. 2:7

Jimmie Nelson is Professor of Preaching and Associate Dean, the Doctor of Ministry Degree Program at Southwestern Baptist Theological Seminary in Fort Worth, Texas.

PREPARING FOR PEOPLE OF OTHER PERSUASIONS

    The young woman seated next to me on the plane was looking out the window. Her name tag indicated she was a Mormon missionary. I started the conversation by asking "Isn't your name from the book of Mormon?" "Well yes," she replied. We talked for the next twenty minutes about Latter-day Saints and the mission trip she was finishing in the Southeast. She was excited to be returning to her home in Texas.
    The conversation had been friendly and dealt with Mormon beliefs, so she asked "How long have you been a Latter-day Saint?" I smiled at the Lord's timing and responded "I'm not, but I studied the book of Mormon as a young man searching for God. Through that study of the world's religions I discovered the teachings of Jesus and became His follower. When I studied your faith I discovered that my beliefs as a Christian are pretty different from yours." With absolute innocence she asked "Oh really, how do they differ?" We spent the next hour talking about the differences between biblical Christianity and Mormon teachings. She mentioned she had developed a friendship with a Baptist on her field. Her

Baptist friend also had shared with her about a personal relationship with Jesus.

As the plane was landing she acknowledged three things. First, she agreed that I am a Christian. Most Mormons do not believe non-Mormons are saved. Second, she agreed to read non-Mormon writers about Christianity. Finally, she agreed to read non-Mormon writers about Mormonism. If she has done those last two things, she may be a believer today. We later discovered she mistakenly had not taken her assigned seat! Her error had not been discovered since the plane was not full. The rest of the morning I evaluated our discussion and thought of things I might have said that could have brought closure to her decision.

Principles of Preparing for People of other Persuasions

This story illustrates several lessons for this chapter.

1. The Holy Spirit is active in the life of believers and unbelievers to set "divine appointments."
2. Every believer must be prepared to meet and respond to people of other religious persuasions.
3. Witnessing dialogue usually should be intentionally evangelistic without being antagonistic.
4. People of other persuasions are open to clear, friendly presentations of the Gospel.
5. Every witness is one link in a Spirit-initiated chain of search and discovery that leads individuals to faith in Jesus Christ.
6. Witnessing is a skill that requires practice. We can often end a witnessing encounter and later think of things we should have said or done.
7. Most false religions use the same vocabulary used by Christians but often have radical differences in definition. Their definitions differ on such key words as salvation, conversion, God, sin, heaven, hell, church, and the Holy Spirit.

This chapter briefly examines the beliefs and biblical response to four of the most common religious persuasions you will encounter: Mormonism, Catholicism, Judaism, and American Islam, plus consideration of other cults. A thorough awareness of this information will help prepare you to effectively share the Gospel with people of othe persuasions.

People of the Mormon Persuasion

Two Mormon missionaries came to my door on a Saturday morning. I invited them in and listened to their presentations. Brian was new to his mission and was being trained by an Elder who was soon to return to Utah.

They asked if I had any questions. I did. I asked about the differences between biblical Christianity and Mormon teachings. The older Elder tried to answer all the questions. Brian was looking up the verses I was asking about. I shared my testimony.

Then surprisingly Brian asked "So you have a personal relationship with Jesus?" Almost immediately the older Elder thanked me for the time and said they had to leave. I walked with them out the door answering Brian's question. At the mailbox I invited them back. Brian said, "thank you for being so nice to us." They never came back.

Many Mormons, like people of any persuasion, are more cultural members rather than actual converts. As a cultural member they grew up in the religious persuasion. They may know the vocabulary and accepted behavior without having a scriptural or spiritual basis for their belief. Cultural Mormons are open to a presentation of the gospel. At the same time, Mormons know about cultural Christians and target them for conversion to Mormonism.

The official name for Mormons is the Church of Jesus Christ of Latter-day Saints (LDS). It was founded in 1830 by Joseph Smith Jr. The headquarters is in Salt Lake City, Utah. In 1995 they had 47,311 missionaries and 8.9 million members worldwide. About half (4.5 million) of that number are in the United States.

Since 1830 more than 100 groups have split from the "true" church. The largest of these splinter groups is the Reorganized Church of Jesus Christ of Latter Day Saints. Their headquarters is in Independence, Missouri.[1]

Mormons are probably best known for their Mormon Tabernacle Choir, missionary teams and excellent television commercials. The commercials have been very effective in improving their general acceptance by positioning themselves on popular family issues. Mormons attempt to show themselves as a traditional, biblical denomination. However, even a cursory look at their teachings show they are a false religion. Remember, though, that many of the Mormons you will meet on the field will not be as aware of these teachings as you are about to be. They have joined the Mormon church because of family tradition or the excellent "sales job" done by the missionaries.

The Southern Baptist Home Mission Board's "Interfaith Witness Belief Bulletin, Mormons" presents basic Mormon doctrines and biblical responses. Mormon doctrine teaches that God always reveals His will through prophets as shown in Amos 3:7 and Malachi 3:6. That statement can be readily accepted by Christians. However, the Mormons then go on to say that God reveals His will today only through the Mormon prophet. That prophet is the leader of the Mormon church. He can receive revelation on any temporal or spiritual matter that **must be accepted as new scripture** by faithful Mormons. They also teach a person cannot receive "godhood" unless they accept Joseph Smith as a Prophet. See how they take truth as a lure then wrap it in falsehood.

The Christian response should be to verify that a true prophet's teaching agrees with the revelation of Jesus Christ (1 Cor. 14:29; Heb. 1:1-3.) God reveals His will today through the Scriptures.

A second Mormon doctrine indicates the need for four sets of accepted scripture. The King James Version of the Bible is the LDS church's official version, but is accepted as the Word of God only "as far as it is correctly translated." Joseph Smith made more than 600 "corrections" to the KJV text. In Mormon teaching the Bible is not complete in its revelation, nor is it the final written authority. Their three additional scriptures are: *The Book of Mormon, Another Testament of Jesus Christ; The Doctrine and Covenants*; and *The Pearl of Great Price*. The *Book of Mormon* claims to be the "fullness of the gospel" and "the most correct of any book on earth." It was supposedly translated by Joseph Smith from gold plates shown to him by the angel Moroni. Incidentally, the *Book of Mormon* has never been able to withstand the kind of historical scrutiny that the Bible has endured. *The Pearl of Great Price* contains Smith's "correction" of Genesis 1-6 and Matthew 24, the account of his first vision, the book of Abraham, and the thirteen Articles of Faith. *The Doctrines and Covenants* contains 138 revelations and two "declarations" and is considered important for doctrinal training.[2]

Christians believe the Bible is the authoritative Word of God. Any "new" revelation cannot contradict what He has already revealed in the Scriptures (2 Tim. 3:15-17; 2 Pet. 1:19-21). The Bible warns about those who preach "another gospel" (Gal 1:6-9).

A third doctrine of Mormonism is that God is an exalted man. They believe there are an infinite number of gods in the universe, each of whom is the god of his own planet. God the Heavenly Father is separate and distinct from Jesus Christ and the Holy Ghost. God the Heavenly Father lived on a planet as a mortal man before attaining "godhood" or "exaltation."

The Bible teaches there is only one true God (Deut. 6:4; Isa. 43:10, 44:6-8; John 10:30, 17:3; 1 Tim 2:5). God cannot be likened to anyone or anything on earth (Isa. 40:18).

There are numerous other false teachings in Mormonism listed in this "Belief Bulletin". These show conclusively that Mormonism is not another mainline denomination but is a false religion. The "Belief Bulletin" presents 14 General Guidelines for Effective Interfaith Witness: (1) Develop a clear understanding of your faith and the Bible; (2) Gain a basic knowledge of Mormon doctrine, especially their "pet" arguments; (3) Make a list of Scriptures that refute their claims; memorize them, and keep them in your Bible; (4) Witness first to your Mormon neighbor or friend, not a missionary; (5) Keep the initiative in the encounter; (6) Ask for and give clear definitions of all terms; (7) Don't allow a Mormon to use the Bible as a 'hook' to distract you before he moves to a Mormon teaching; (8) Check that every biblical text is correctly cited and always consider its context; (9) Center the discussion on basic Christian doctrines and don't get sidetracked defending your denomination; (10) Remember, just because a Mormon 'testifies' something is true does not make it so; (11) Point out the danger of relying on feelings; emphasize that the Bible is a more reliable guide than feelings; (12) Give a strong, positive testimony of your salvation experience; (13) Pray for God's love and patience; winning a Mormon takes time; and (14) Trust the Holy Spirit to lead you.[3]

People of the Catholic Persuasion

Willie and Myrna were raised Roman Catholic in the Philippines. When they moved to Southern California they continued to do everything their faith told them to do. They attended Mass, went to confession, and were "good" people. One day they were given a Bible in their heart language (the language they grew up using) by door-to-door visitors from a local Baptist church. Willie says "I was a good person. I did all the right things. But I had no peace. I did not accept Jesus until I read His word and understood His life, teachings, and resurrection. The Bible showed me that Jesus is the only way to God. Myrna also accepted Jesus when she read for herself what Jesus did for us. We are so grateful that someone gave us a Bible we can read and understand."

Many people, not just Catholics, believe that being *good* is what God expects of us. They are surprised to learn that being good is not enough. The prerequisite to attain eternal life is to become holy. The only way we become holy is to ask God's Holy Spirit to come live inside of us. Then we are transformed into new creatures, we are reborn.

Many people in the Catholic persuasion rely on this "salvation by works." The "Interfaith Witness Belief Bulletin, Catholicism" presents introductory information on Catholic beliefs and the biblical response.

The Roman Catholic Church reports a 1991 global membership of 850 million, with 58 million of those living in the U.S. The world headquarters is the Vatican in Rome, Italy. U.S. headquarters is in Washington, D.C. The church traces its history to Jesus as the founder and to Peter as the first in a line of 262 popes. Protestant historians date the Catholic Church to the fifth and sixth centuries. The word "Catholic" means "universal" and for 1500 years the Western World was predominantly Catholic.[4]

Eastern Orthodox Catholics split from Roman Catholicism in 1054 over differences in beliefs and practices. They recognize seven essential bearers of the grace of God: (1) Triple immersion baptism; (2) Confirmation by anointing; (3) Confession; (4) Holy Communion; (5) Holy Orders; (6) Holy Matrimony; and (7) Last Rites. With six million members in the Americas, they are not as common as Roman Catholics or other persuasions discussed in this chapter.[5]

One of the primary doctrinal differences between Catholics and Protestants concerns Mary. Catholic teaching asserts that Mary was conceived without original sin, and remained a virgin throughout her life. An important distinction in the Catholic theology of Mary is the assertion that she is the mother of God. As such, she cooperated in the redemption of humankind and even is sometimes called co-mediatrix (also serves as our mediator with God). Protestants believe in the biblical view of Jesus being the only mediator between God and man. (1 Tim. 2:5)

A second great distinction between Catholics and Protestants is the doctrine of salvation. Daniel Sanchez writes "The Catholic Church teaches that salvation is uncertain, mediated and sacramental. In contrast, evangelicals base their concept of salvation on the Scripture verses . . . which teach that we can be (certain) of our salvation; that our salvation is (personal) (We can go directly to Christ, our Mediator); and that salvation is by grace through (faith) in Christ and not through sacraments." [6] The evangelical response includes John 3:16, 5:24, 10:9-10, Eph. 2:8-9, and the verse that haunted Martin Luther, Romans 1:17. Sanchez's materials provide excellent information on sharing with Catholics.

The "Belief Bulletin" offers this list of Guidelines: (1) Have a clear understanding of your faith; (2) Have a basic knowledge of Roman Catholic theology; (3) Avoid the tendency to argue about matters of faith, rather, share your faith with gentleness and love; (4) Stress the approachability and understanding of God as evidenced in Jesus; (5) Stress the competence of individuals to respond to God's revelation through the guidance of the Holy Spirit; (6) Point out the importance of an individual making a conscious decision to follow Christ at some stage in his or her religious pilgrimage; (7) Explain how the pilgrimage of the Christian life revolves around. . . trust and commitment; and (8) Stress that continued trust and commitment bring assurance of salvation.[7]

People of the Jewish Persuasion

I stood at the wailing wall in Jerusalem and watched devout, committed Jews rock back and forth toward the wall in an attempt to communicate with God. Small slips of paper were slid between the massive stones of the wall that was all that remained of their house for God. The note I slid between the rocks contained a heartfelt prayer that had already been carried by the Spirit to the throne. It read "Oh great Jehovah, bring Your peace to Jerusalem through a revival that opens their eyes to Your Messiah."

In a suburb of Atlanta, Ga., Conservative Jews buy homes within walking distance of the temple so they can remain obedient to the Law. Jewish parents brought their Children to the Baptist daycare because of the quality of the education. Most workers were surprised to find such a strong, well-organized Jewish community in the heart of the Bible Belt. You will encounter people of the Jewish persuasion in most of the places where you serve.

Bob Adams writes, "Jews, like Baptists are individuals; speaking about all Jews has the same degree of validity as speaking generally about *the Baptists*... Only as we consistently relate to Jews as friends, only as we deliberately break down the barriers that separate us will any real dialogue occur."[8] Being a friend is important for sharing our faith with people of any religious persuasion. Our urgency and sincerity increases when we are dealing with the welfare and conversion of a friend from another persuasion.

Many Christians are familiar with the beliefs of our Jewish ancestry. Judaism began with Abraham in the Middle East about 1800 B.C. It was the first world religion to emphasize monotheism--the belief in one creator God who revealed His will to His people. Jews strongly saw themselves as God's instruments for blessing the world.

Their bible, called Tanach, contains what Christians call the Old Testament. God's will was outlined in the Ten Commandments and expanded first in the Hebrew Scriptures and later in the Talmud. The Talmud is an extensive commentary on Tanach. In addition to Tanach and Talmud there is Torah. Professor Jacob Neusner notes that for nearly a millennium Torah had meant a particular scroll or book. In *Foundations of Judaism* he writes of the change that has occurred among Jews in reference to Torah, "When a rabbi spoke of Torah, he no longer meant only a particular object, a scroll and its contents. Now he used the word to encompass a distinctive and well-defined worldview and way of life. Torah now stood for something one does."[9]

Neusner's quote is important to those who are witnessing to people of the Jewish persuasion. Many Jews see themselves more as a cultural group than as a religious group. The witness needs to be sensitive. The person should be able to accept Christ as Messiah without giving up their cultural heritage.

Simon was an Orthodox Jew living in Florida. He was very intelligent, in his late thirties, and responsive to our discussion that Jesus is the Messiah. He examined the New Testament verses and could quote many of the Old Testament texts I mentioned. He became very animated as he led the conversation to the Holocaust and the creation of the modern state of Israel. He was a fervent Zionist, not understanding the difference between biblical Zion and modern Israel. His cultural identity was tied to being a Jew. He could not fathom how to become a Christian believer and still remain a cultural Jew. I showed him, through the Spirit's guidance, that this was the same dilemma faced by the Jerusalem Council in Acts 15. He saw for the first time in his life that he did not have to become a Gentile to believe in the Messiah. Simon believed Christians had completely reversed the first century problem of requiring Gentiles to become Jews before they could become Christians!

The Jewish sacrificial system practiced in the Old Testament changed with the diaspora. Jews had dispersed to every corner of the world by the time the Temple was destroyed in 70 A.D. Rabbinic Judaism developed as many of the religious duties of worship and prayer were transferred to the Synagogues."[10]

There are three primary branches of Judaism. Orthodox Judaism is tradition oriented and strictly adheres to the Talmud. Reform Judaism dates from the nineteenth century in Europe and does not adhere as strictly to the Talmud, particularly in terms of food and food preparation. Orthodox Jews believe in Heaven and Hell, but reform Judaism would not assert any life beyond this one. Conservative Judaism is a North American response that mediates the strictness of Orthodox Judaism and the liberality of the reform Jews.

Guidelines for sharing Christ with a person of the Jewish persuasion are consistent with the guidelines listed for other persuasions. Know the historical roots of Christianity. Become familiar with Old and New Testament references to Jesus as the Messiah. Remain focused on Jesus. Do not get led into a discussion of Zionism or the Holocaust. Be kind and firm. Do not attack Judaism but show its fulfillment in Christ.

You may want to host special services at your church in conjunction with Jewish holidays. Church members may enjoy learning about our Jewish heritage. They may likewise feel comfortable inviting their Jewish friends to a Christian celebration out of respect for their holidays. A Passover celebration can add meaning to Easter celebrations, as does a Hanukkah celebration at Christmas.

People of the American Islam Persuasion

The three of us entered the Mosque with fear and trembling. Surely these were all Moslem extremists preparing a bomb for some innocent target in the Los Angeles area. We were greeted warmly and given friendly instructions how to observe their worship and prayers.

Afterwards we were invited to eat with the worshipers. The lamb was spicy and delicious. A young Black man came and sat with us. He shared his testimony of how Islam had changed his life. He told of his early life in drugs and gangs. He met *Allah* and began to follow the teachings of the Qu'ran (Koran). He then probed to see if he could help us know *Allah*.

I responded that we were followers of the Prophet Isa, the name for Jesus in the Qu'ran. As we talked about the teachings of Jesus, a small group gathered at the table. They peppered us with questions that indicated they had no idea of Christian teachings. They were very interested in the differences in the teachings of Christianity and Islam.

Suddenly, and simultaneously the Spirit warned us it was time to go. As we stood to leave we noticed a small group of leaders huddled by the door behind us and gesturing in our direction. Only then did our new-found friends begin to look anxious. They literally surrounded us in a gesture of protectiveness, ushered us out the door and to the car. I gave one the New Testament I was carrying. He said, "We will seek the teachings of Isa."

Muslims (or Moslems) are often radically missionary adherents to the world religion of Islam. Estimates of worldwide population average 800 million to 1 billion adherents. The United States accounts for 4-6 million of that number. The word Islam means "submission." Their aim is for all humanity to submit to God. The crescent moon symbol was adopted when Muslims chose the lunar calendar to measure time. Islam is growing rapidly and you will probably encounter Muslims in your wherever you serve.[11]

The "Interfaith Witness Belief Bulletin, Islam" presents a clear picture of Islam and the biblical response. The leader of Islam is Muhammed (Mohammed). He founded Islam in 622 A.D. to confront paganism with his assertion that God is one. He unified all of Arabia with this teaching and laid the foundation for global evangelization to their cause. He is considered the "seal of the prophets" and the messenger of God who brought God's final revelation to the world.

You can see here another common factor in false religions. Each of them claim to bring additional revelation from God. The authority of the Christian Bible is based on the unique resurrection of Jesus Christ. The Biblical claims of sufficiency are validated by Jesus. No additional revelation is needed for humankind to meet and have a relationship with the Creator. Muslims also deny the resurrection of Jesus.

The sacred book of Islam is the Qu'ran. It is understood by Muslims to be the precise word of God given to Muhammed by the angel Gabriel (Jibril). It is considered the final and perfect revelation of God. (See the similarities to other false religions?) It is shorter than the New Testament and is divided into 114 chapters called Suras. Islam asserts the Qu'ran is the only divinely revealed scripture that has been preserved in its exact original form throughout history.

The framework for Muslim life and practice is found in the "Five Pillars." (1) Faith. The faithful pronounce "There is no God except God, and Muhammed is the messenger of God." Muslims often accuse Christians of worshiping three Gods because of our emphasis on the Trinity. (2) Prayer. Required five times a day. The prescribed prayers are in Arabic, the language of the Qu'ran. (3) Almsgiving. Muslims believe that possessions are purified by setting aside a portion for those in need. This involves the payment each year of 2.5 percent of one's capital wealth. (4) The Fast. Seen as a method of self-purification, it occurs each year during the month of Ramadan. The faithful abstain from food, drink, and sex between sunup to sundown. The monetary value of the food or the food that would have been consumed is given to the poor. (5) Pilgrimage. An annual trip to Mecca is only required for those who physically and financially are able to make it. Everyone wears simple clothing to stand equal before God.

There are a growing number of mosques in the United States. George Braswell writes, "The mosque is the symbol of unity and universality in Islam. The leader of the mosque is the *Imam* who serves as the model for the Muslim lifestyle. The *Imam* interprets the law of Islam through sermons and classes."[12]

There is a distinction between Islam and the Nation of Islam. Glen Igleheart explains: "The Nation of Islam was a black separatist movement that was both anti-white and anti-Christian. Its black supremacy view taught Allah was black, and all human beings were originally black. Whites and other races were created through selective breeding by a mad scientist named Yakub. Whites, therefore, were devils."[13] The Moslem ethics provided a rigid code of conduct and a sense of identity. The most famous convert in the past was Malcolm X and today, Louis Farrakhan. The last name of X was acquired to give up the old name from his or her days of slavery. Then an Arabic name is taken.

The "Belief Bulletin" presents five "Guidelines For Witnessing to Muslims:

(1) Recognize that Islam teaches some ideas with which you as a Christian can agree. Whenever possible, let these ideas be points of contact that the Holy Spirit can use to bless your relationship with Muslims. Affirm to your Muslim neighbors how you believe that God (Allah) is One, God is Creator, God is sovereign. Affirm how you believe that God reveals Himself and His will, and that He wants us to respond to Him in faith and 'submission.'

(2) Be willing to acknowledge points of agreement . . . such as the general concepts of angels and life after death. You can also indicate respect for the worship, fasting, and almsgiving of Muslims and their sense of peoplehood and unity. But point out to Muslim acquaintances that there are also clear points of contradiction between Islam and Christianity, such as the roles of Jesus and Muhammed, the role of the Qu'ran, the sufficiency of God's revelation in Jesus.

(3) Recognize that there are both similarities and differences between the Muslim and the Christian understandings of sin and salvation. Ask your Muslim acquaintances to consider the life and death of Jesus as God's finest demonstration of His mercy and grace. To Muslims sin is disobedience of responsible human beings to the law of Almighty God. Sin is caused by human weakness, by forgetfulness, and by a spirit of rebellion. Christians believe that human beings have chosen to sin against God, rejecting His nature and pursuing a course of life that is opposed to God's essential character and revealed law. Human beings need to be 'saved,' rescued from their persistent indifference and hostility toward God. They are unable by their own efforts to achieve genuine righteousness and a right relationship with God. Christians believe that individuals can receive forgiveness for sin and restoration to fellowship with God through faith in the merit of Jesus. Christians further believe that deeds of worship and service follow and grow out of the Christian's faith in Jesus: those deeds are not efforts to earn God's favor.

(4) Deal graciously with a Muslim's objections to, or misunderstandings of, Christian beliefs and practices (if Muslims bring up these issues). Clarify any misunderstandings that exist and work seriously at reducing animosities and distortions about both Islam and Christianity.

(5) Introduce Muslims to the Bible with clarity and sensitivity. Muslims generally distrust the Bible and are often confused about its stories, events, and terms. Help them become familiar with the Bible; show them how to read it; invite them to read it with you. (Begin with the Gospel of Luke). Let the Holy Spirit validate the Bible as you refer to it reverently and leave it in the hands of an inquiring Muslim."[14]

(6) I would add to this list that we need to be careful not to approach a person from the Middle East with prejudicial biases. Fundamentalist Muslims practice a characteristic combativeness, exclusivism, and closed-mindedness that are considered dangerous by other Muslims. A relationship with Jesus Christ is the only solution to contemporary terrorism and radical claims that do not represent the revelation of God.

People of Cultic Persuasions

The young woman wore a T-shirt that read "Orthodox Druid." She considered herself an earth-worshipper and was hostile to the claims of Christianity.

Linda has brochures that describe her as a "Certified Crystal Healer." She does workshops to teach inner healing and stress-reduction. Her workshops [at $75 an hour] encompass channelled information about the crystals; energy and Chakra balancing; cleansing and charging your personal stones, and sharing methods you may use for your personal enrichment. She works with "Ascended Masters" to guide her in healing layouts.

Jim Jones and David Koresh led their followers to mass suicides and murder.

Carrie believed that her own intellect could discern right from wrong. She led a self-destructive lifestyle with no semblance to Judeo-Christian morals or values. She cursed me and tried to have me reject her. Then she tried seduction. She quoted Shakespeare and popular songs in attempts to define her philosophy of life. She knew she was a humanist but she had no knowledge of Scripture and had never attended any church, not even for a wedding or funeral. She was miserable and though she kept trying to divert our discussion she would come back again and again to the question, how do we know God. That is the question posed by many of the millions of people in the cultic persuasion. Christians have the answer to that question through a relationship with Jesus Christ.

A simple definition of a cult is a false religion. Religion can be defined as humans seeking God. Christianity, however, is God seeking humankind. Cults are non-biblical systems that humans create in an attempt to find God. Many American cults claim some affiliation to Christianity. They target people who have spiritual interest but are biblically illiterate. These counterfeit religions provide a semblance of religion with no true substance. The Southern Baptist Home Mission Board Interfaith Witness Department research files include information about more than 500 cults in the U.S.

Cults should not be confused with the occult. The word occult means "hidden" and there are three categories of occultism: (1) "fortune-telling (foreseeing the future or perceiving human character through extra-sensory means); (2) magic (effecting results through supernatural powers); and (3) Spiritism (contacting the dead or receiving other revelations from beyond this life)." The occult is often tied to Satan worship and is also on the rise in the U.S.[15]

The "Interfaith Witness Belief Bulletin, Cult/Sect Overview" presents three types of Cults and Sects: (1) "Millennial Groups. These groups emphasize the end of the world, Christ's return, and the coming judgement of all non-members. Salvation is attained through works within the group. Examples of millennial cults are Jehovah's Witnesses, the Church of Jesus Christ of Latter-day Saints (Mormons), and the Church of God International. The many other lesser-known millennial groups are particularly active during the years leading to the change of the millennium. (2) Mind Groups. These groups emphasize human potential and the importance of the mind in religion. Salvation comes through knowledge. These groups borrow doctrines from non-Christian world religions such as Hinduism, while claiming to be Christian. Christian Science and the Unity School of Christianity are examples. (3) East-West Mixes. These groups do not claim Christianity as the primary parent faith, but many incorporate Christian teachings in their belief systems. Examples include Hare Krishna and Transcendental Meditation, which identify Hinduism as the parent faith, and Scientology, which claims to be the fulfillment of Buddhism."[16]

The cults are so numerous and so diverse that it is impossible to present a brief overview of their teachings. The easiest way to be prepared is to be able to identify the characteristics of a cult. You will encounter many people from cultic persuasions where you serve. Be prepared to respond to them, and to their families, in general terms when they ask you about any particular cult. The "Belief Bulletin" presents five major characteristics of a cult or sect.

(1) A Single Charismatic Leader or Authority Figure. This person is the sole source of revelation from God; he or she becomes the primal authority for theology and biblical interpretation. Salvation is attained by following the teachings of the leader who claims special relationship with God, fulfilling the role of a biblical prophet, apostle, or messiah. The president of the Mormon Church is called "prophet, seer, and revelator." Sun Myung Moon to his followers is the messiah who has come to complete Jesus' failed mission.

(2) Belief in Supplemental Revelation. New revelations, which supersede and contradict previous revelations, are received through the leader and accepted as new teachings from God. The Mormon teaching that God was once a man is a new revelation.

(3) Acceptance of New Written Authority. New scriptures or authoritative works, which supersede the Bible or are necessary to correctly interpret the Bible, are accepted. The leader may claim to have discovered a "key" to correctly interpret the Bible or "errors" in the biblical text. Mary Baker Eddy's *Science and Health with Key to the Scriptures* is used by Christian Scientists as their "key." *The Book of Mormon* is an example of new scripture.

(4) Belief That the Group Is the One True Church. A cult claims to be God's one true organization with a living leader, to have new truth from God, and/or to know the correct interpretation of the Bible. Historic Christianity is rejected.

(5) Changed Theology. Cults advocate a new theology through their belief in supplemental revelation or biblical interpretation by the leader. Often traditional Christian terms are redefined. This change or deviation centers in the person and work of Jesus Christ and usually includes the authority of the Bible and doctrines of the Trinity, humankind, and salvation. Jehovah's Witnesses, for example, reject the Trinity, the personality of the Holy Spirit, and the divinity and physical resurrection of Christ."[17]

Learn these five characteristics or write them in your Bible or calendar. Begin to walk circumspectly as you see the faith of those you encounter. These characteristics apply in many, often surprising, situations. It is disconcerting to see how many television preachers qualify under one or more of these characteristics.

Also be careful of cultic tendencies in your own ministry. The strong personality types that characterize some ministers also characterize cultic groups when spiritual gifts are misused.

The guidelines for witnessing to people of other sects and cults are similar to guidelines from each persuasion in this chapter. Know the biblical foundation for what you believe, share your testimony, stay on the important issues, share the truth in love, and rely on the Holy Spirit.

Conclusion

You will discover the primary persuasions where you serve when you study the demographics of your field. The phone book is a ready resource to discover the main churches in your area. The cults will be harder to determine.

The basic issue in dealing with people in other persuasions is your individual, personal relationship with the Lord Jesus. Begin each day with prayer and Bible Study. You will be amazed how often you have opportunities to use what you have just studied. Seek to be a "straw" for the Spirit's use--clean and pliable, filled with His love. Take comfort that any success, recognition, or praise are for what comes through the straw.

When you have put on the spiritual armor, work hard. Pray for divine appointments. Take advantage of every "chance encounter." Set a goal to share your faith every day and to lead someone to Jesus at least once a week. Conversion growth is the most significant contribution you can make where you serve. Become responsible for reducing the population of Hell.

Newly appointed missionaries have told me that their most significant contribution is to reduce human suffering or to meet needs. That is certainly part of our ministry, but it is a means to effective, person-centered evangelism. Evangelism is not limited to those who have the gift of the evangelist. Neither is ministry limited to those with the gift of helps. Jesus came "to save that which was lost" (Matt. 18:11). Be careful that your focus is consistent with Christ's mission. People of other persuasions are lost without Jesus Christ. He is "the Way, and the Truth, and the Life (John 14:6)." Now it's up to you. In our secular culture you will be the only Christian that some of these people will ever have talked to. Be prepared, take the initiative, and rely on the Holy Spirit.

Endnotes

1. Gary Leazer, "Latter-day Saints," in *Beliefs of Other Kinds*, (Atlanta: Home Mission Board, 1984), pp. 73-74.

2. Gary Leazer, "Interfaith Witness Belief Bulletin, Mormons," (Atlanta: Home Mission Board, SBC, 1990), p. 2.

3. Ibid. p. 4.

4. Richard W. Harmon, "Interfaith Witness Belief Bulletin, Roman Catholics," (Atlanta: Home Mission Board, SBC, 1985), p. 1.

5. Homer Goumenis, "Eastern Orthodox," in *Beliefs of Other Kinds*, (Atlanta: Home Mission Board, 1984), pp. 41-46.

6. Daniel R. Sanchez, *Sharing our Faith with Roman Catholic Friends*, (Atlanta: Home Mission Board, SBC, 1992), p. 24.

7. Harmon, p. 4.

8. Bob E. Adams, "Judaism," in *Beliefs of Other Kinds*, (Atlanta: Home Mission Board, 1984), pp. 104-114.

9. Jacob Neusner, *Foundations of Judaism*, (Philadelphia:Fortress Press, 1989), p. 3.

10. Glen Igleheart, "Interfaith Witness Belief Bulletin, World Religions Overview," (Atlanta: Home Mission Board, 1984), p. 2.

11. Maurice Smith, "Interfaith Witness Belief Bulletin, Islam," (Atlanta: Home Mission Board, 1990), pp. 1-4.

12. George W. Braswell, Jr., "Islam," in *Beliefs of Other Kinds*, (Atlanta: Home Mission Board, 1984), pp. 121-125.

13. Glen Igleheart, "American Black Muslims," in *Beliefs of Other Kinds*, (Atlanta: Home Mission Board, 1984), pp. 126-127.

14. Smith, p. 4.

15. George Sheridan, "The Occult," in *Beliefs of Other Kinds*, (Atlanta: Home Mission Board, 1984), p. 120.

16. Gary Leazer, "Interfaith Witness Belief Bulletin, Cult/Sect Overview," (Atlanta: Home Mission Board, 1983, 1990), pp. 1-2.

17. Cult/Sect Overview, p. 4.

C. Thomas Wright is the Director of Materials Development for the Evangelism Section of the Southern Baptist Home Mission Board, Atlanta, Georgia. A former missionary Journeyman to Thailand, he served with the Home Mission Board's Language Church Extension prior to coming to the Evangelism Section.

Preparing to Witness to Strangers

I put on righteousness as my clothing;
justice was my robe and turban.
I was eyes to the blind
and feet to the lame.
I was a father to the needy;
I took up the case of the stranger.

— Job 29:14-16

    A carnival of sights and sounds fills the street called Bourbon. Terry, a young man, is captivated by the voluptuous intrigue of song and dance. He peers eagerly through a narrow dance hall door seeking to satisfy his taste for the night life. He laughs and tells his friends how free he feels and how much he loves the life he lives.

    Three days a week Sherry works carrying out groceries for the customers who shop at her store. She is polite, but seldom has much to say. When she is not thinking about work, she is thinking about her new baby at home with his grandmother. Life as a single mom is hard and she works just to make ends meet.

John and Barbara Powers live on Mission Street in a small suburban town some forty-five minutes from downtown. They leave in the morning by seven and return in the evening around six-thirty. They have not met many of their neighbors. Always on the go, the Powers have no time for chit-chat or courteous salutations. Driven by dreams of success, their careers must come first.

The people mentioned above represent the *strangers* who anonymously share our lives. Wherever we are, from the familiar surroundings of our own neighborhoods and grocery stores, to the public places we visit while on vacation, we encounter people we do not know. Who are these nameless faces? Do we have something that they need? What is it to, "take up the case of the stranger"?

Evangelical Christians have a commission to "take" the Gospel to all persons. This charge includes those we call strangers. A greeting or an act of kindness may provide an opportunity to meet a stranger. Being *prepared* will help you to move beyond an introduction into an opportunity to share your faith. Being prepared helps build bridges and dissolve barriers. So, how can you prepare to witness to a stranger?

Like athletes training for an upcoming relay, *how well prepared Christians are for witnessing is measured primarily by their prior conditioning.* Conditioning is both a short-term and a long-term endeavor. Short-term conditioning includes planning, prayer, knowledge of the cultural setting, an attitude of care, and a willingness to help.

Long-term conditioning is the focus of this chapter and includes: *knowing God, knowing yourself, knowing what you believe, and knowing people.* As you mature in these areas you will become more secure in your witnessing. Boldness and confidence will replace fear and apprehension. You will seize opportunities to witness—anywhere, anytime, and to anyone. The notion of a "right" way to witness will give way to an inspired, natural way of sharing.

Being prepared leads to many different witnessing opportunities *naturally*. Witnessing becomes an extension of the way you live and is no longer a program that must be planned out in order for it to occur. Reluctancy, caused by shaming expectations, insecurity, guilt, and fear is reduced. Desire is increased. You act on what you know at the time. You are no longer left feeling wounded or defeated, second guessing yourself with such questions as:

"Did I do all I could have?"

"Did I say the "right" thing?"

"Did I thwart someone's opportunity to be saved by not answering a question the way I now think I should have?"

"Should I have tried a little harder?"

"Did I use the "right" Scripture?"

Additionally, the trappings of expecting a certain response from the other person are avoided. Genuiness and integrity are conveyed. *Authenticity occurs when the one who is witnessing focuses on a compassionate presence that invites the other person to move closer to Christ.*

Long-term conditioning prepares you to receive the work of the Holy Spirit. The Holy Spirit acts as a silent partner in the encounter. Through the Spirit, you may experience one or several of the following:

unusual awareness

unusual boldness

unusual peace in the midst of

harassment or hostility

unusual satisfaction as the encounter

closes (whatever the outcome may be)

Provisions such as these sustain, encourage, and guide the encounter and help develop confidence for future witnessing opportunities. Being prepared to witness to strangers begins with knowing God.

Knowing God

J.I. Packer has stated that humankind was made to know God.[1] However, there is a vast difference between knowing God and knowing *about* God.[2] Focusing on this point Packer asserts "one can know a great deal about God without much knowledge of Him." He wrote,

> I am sure that many of us have never grasped this. We find in ourselves a deep interest in theology . . . . We read books of theological exposition and apologetics. We dip into Christian history, and study the Christian creed. We learn to find our way around in

the Scriptures. Others appreciate our interest in these things, and we find ourselves asked to give our opinion in public on this or that Christian question, to lead study groups, to give papers, to write articles, and generally to accept responsibility, informal if not formal, for acting as teachers and arbiters of orthodoxy in our own Christian circle. Our friends tell us how much they value our contribution, and this spurs us to further explorations of God's truth, so that we may be equal to the demands made upon us. All very fine—yet interest in theology, and knowledge about God, and the capacity to think clearly and talk well on Christian themes, is not at all the same thing as knowing Him.[3]

Knowing God occurs through on-going personal and relational experiences with God. It is the continuous internal change of an individual which brings about a natural and continuous external change. This is the on-going purposed plunge into the person of Christ, resulting in the reckless abandonment of self-centeredness, self-servitude, and self-promotion.[4]

The person who has known God and is knowing God is determined to act and react in ways that are characteristic of Christ.[5] Knowing God means giving priority to changing your "being" (i.e. thinking, feeling, and believing) over your behavior. The Christian is not overwhelmed with doing the *right* things but places priority on being the *right* person, believing that good doing comes from a godly being. The result of such a change is true piety, humility, empathy, and compassion.

True piety distinguishes the believer from what is typically experienced by the stranger.[6] The stranger recognizes an inviting difference. Humility conveys sincerity. Empathy conveys a sense of genuine interest and a willingness to identify with the stranger's plight. Compassion communicates a readiness to help, to serve, and to support in tangible as well as spiritual ways.

Preparing to witness to strangers also includes a better understanding of yourself. A direct correlation exists between how well you minister to others and how well you know yourself.

Knowing Yourself

The study of self is a necessary and intrinsic part of long-term conditioning. "How many of us have learned to look inwardly with courage? We have to get rid of the idea that we understand ourselves. This is always the last bit of pride to go."[7]

It is astounding to notice how ignorant people are about themselves. Typically, it is a crisis or an occasion for counseling when individuals seek an in-depth study of themselves. Why is this? Part of the answer lies in the distortion of some Christian teachings on the subject of self.

Getting to know yourself and using that information to make improvements is consistent with biblical teaching. When Christ told his disciples that they would know the truth and the truth would set them free (Jn. 8:32), "he was referring not only to an intellectual assent to truth, but also to the application of truth in the most basic issues of life: our goals, our motives, and our sense of self-worth."[8]

The biblical perspective of self is a blending of spiritual and human characteristics. "The human and the divine, the temporal and the eternal are sweetly woven into our lives. Our heavenly attachments and our earthly affairs are so closely related that it is impossible to tell where one ends and the other begins."[9]

Getting to know yourself requires that you be accountable to others. Being accountable to others means you are willing to let others make evaluations about your character. You want to be honest, transparent, and willing to listen. Considering the input of others aids you in the process of personal change.

While there are many facets to the study of self, these questions will help you begin your study:

"What are my spiritual gifts and what do I have a passion to do?"

"What is true of my personality?"

"How can I understand my strengths and weaknesses as a result of what is true of my personality?"

"Who have I become with regard to the history I share with my family and how does that history inform the decisions I make today?"

Answering these questions will enable you to better understand yourself. A discussion of these questions follows, beginning with spiritual gifts.

Exercising spiritual gifts is an essential part of the conditioning which leads to preparedness. As a Christian you possess a unique *gift* from the Holy Spirit.[10] This gift is a character trait that enables you care for and help others. Allocating this gift shapes the attitude and direction of personal and corporate ministry.[11] Spiritual gifts weave Christians together. The "very nature of gifts means that we are all interdependent. No matter how gifted a person may be, he has no life or ministry without the proper working of all other gifts."[12]

By understanding how you are gifted and accessing the passion you have to help others, you can better plan how and where to be the most effective witness. A person with the gift of *mercy,* for instance, might be intimidated in a setting where a person with the gift of *prophecy* is not. Knowing your personality is also a beneficial part of the conditioning that readies you for witnessing.

Getting to know your personality and the many parts linked to such a study is very helpful.[13] For example, knowing you are "choleric" helps you to understand your need to lead, to control, and to have answers quickly. The need to be right is also a common choleric tendency. Understanding how your personality informs the way you interact with others enables you to become a more effective communicator. For example, "if you are Choleric, realize that even though you are usually right, you need to allow others to express opinions without making them feel stupid."[14]

A fascination with analyzing personalities has existed for centuries.[15] Long time educators and believers in personality theory, Fred and Florence Littauer have written, "We have learned that if you give people a tool so simple that they can recognize their strengths, look at their weaknesses, and admit they need to do something about them, they will make the necessary changes."[16] The Littauer's believe that it is not the intellect of a person that brings about life-changing choices; these changes come through their emotions.[17]

You will discover some strengths and weaknesses through a study of your personality. Knowing your strengths and weaknesses better prepares you to effectively communicate and interact with others. Knowing, for instance, that you are phlegmatic and have difficulty making choices, may inspire you to be a better planner. By planning you reduce the potential for conflict related to you being indecisive.

It is common to be interested and, therefore, familiar with strengths while generally avoiding weaknesses. Most of us "don't work on our weaknesses because our faults have been pointed out to us too often by people whose opinions we don't value and whose lives we consider worse than our own."[18] Being familiar with your family history is a third key to better understanding yourself.

A study of family history lends specific and dramatic insight into the makeup of its members.[19] For instance, alcoholism produces insecurity, anger, a need for control, and an unwillingness to take risks among many members who do not drink. This is known as "para-alcoholism" and is a direct result of the influence of the alcoholic.[20] Similar contrasts in behavior can be seen in cases of sexual abuse, substance abuse, and physical abuse. As with the development of a champion thoroughbred over a span of generations, family history silently affects the moulding of its members from generation to generation.[21]

The slogans, "It takes one to know one," "The apple doesn't fall far from the tree," and "He's a chip off the ol' block," all allude to the power of family influence. Family history, often more than you realize, influences your everyday choices. An investigation of both the actual events (e.g. deaths, marriages, separations, divorce, births, careers, education), and the emotional truths (e.g. addictions, abuses, achievements) of your family, reveals what informs the attitudes and behaviors which lie behind the decisions you make.

Knowing yourself helps to lower anxiety, the unconscious exaggeration of personal feelings. When interacting with others, your ability to stay focused on their needs is continuously interrupted by an unconscious awareness of your own needs. You react to what persons say, the way they say it, and to their behavior. Often, the reaction is characterized by increased personal anxiety. When your anxiety increases, your ability to be aware of the other person's feelings and needs decreases. Being less aware of other people's feelings, lowers your ability to minister to them.

Spiritual gifting, personality, and family history combine to determine, in many ways, how persons interact with one another. Being prepared to witness to strangers includes a mature understanding of these components of self. What an individual believes and why they believe what they do is another important part of preparing to witness.

Knowing What You Believe

As a Christian, *what* you believe is crucial to your faith. Learning what you believe takes place, in part, through prayer, studying the Bible, participating in worship, and listening to sermons. As you learn you begin to lay a firm foundation upon which you can continue to build your faith. As you mature in your faith, you will strive to "nail down" what you believe. Knowing *why* you believe what you do is as important as knowing what you believe.

By knowing why you believe as you do, you will be more secure in your faith. You will also be better prepared to share your faith with others. From the Bible, Peter boldly admonishes believers to "always be prepared to give an answer to everyone who asks you to give the reason for the hope that you have."[22]

The *why* of your faith often turns into the substance by which you can answer the skeptic's questions prior to sharing the Gospel. In the book *When Skeptics Ask*, Norman Geisler and Ron Brooks make a case for "pre-evangelism," the answering of objective questions from skeptics.[23] According to these men, "Before we can share the Gospel, we sometimes have to smooth the road . . . and answer the questions that are keeping that person from accepting the Lord."[24]

Finally, knowing people is helpful in preparing to witness to strangers. It is crucial in the development of one's theology and practice of ministry to understand human nature and personal needs.[25]

Knowing People

What you find to be true about yourself, when honesty prevails, you will often find in others. People need more than what they can provide for themselves. At the center of these and other realities is the *universal neediness* of all humankind.

The neediness of people originated as a result of their estrangement from God (a result of sin), and a desperate need to be re-united with their creator (redeemed). "One must understand the biblical doctrine of the human (*anthropos*) in relation to the divine reality (*theos*) in order to understand the nature of sin and redemption."[26]

The Christian view of humankind according to Millard Erickson, "is that man is a creature of God, made in the image of God."[27] Accordingly, the reason for man's existence "lies in the intention of the supreme being."[28] One intention known from Scripture is God's desire to love and be loved. God also intends for persons to love one another. Humans are social beings "placed within society to function in relationships."[29] Relationship implies mutual and personal care, concern, and commitment.[30]

Regarding the knowing of persons, C. W. Brister wrote that some "have become accustomed to thinking of persons in cultural subgroups and to communicating with the masses impersonally in computer form and broadcast fashion."[31] Emphasizing the need to approach people individually and with specific interest Brister wrote, "It takes great effort to see one face in a crowd. It was once observed about a famous American pulpiteer that he loved everyone in general so much that he loved no one in particular."[32]

When you purpose to know God through personal, maturing experiences, seek to know yourself through spiritual gifts, personality, and family history, and get to know people better, you embark on a course of conditioning which leads to a natural preparedness for witnessing. Combining a long-term commitment to preparedness with the unique short-term necessities for witnessing will ensure a greater effectiveness in witnessing to strangers. You are more likely to build rapport with those you meet and convey authenticity and integrity.

Returning now to "Terry," can you imagine how different the encounter with him could be by applying the principles outlined in this chapter? For instance, as a result of you knowing God, you approach Terry with a gentle, caring, inviting presence as opposed to an aggressive approach with a "hard-and-fast" agenda in mind. As a result of knowing yourself better, you are calm and "open" as opposed to anxious and skeptical. You are willing to discuss his views in a spontaneous way instead of becoming defensive and controlling.

When Terry tells you that all things are relative, drawing from what you believe, you can explain the absolute nature of God and discuss why you believe this truth. You can point out that believing all things to be relative is in itself an absolute predisposition.

Knowing people helps you to stay focused on Terry's need for a personal relationship with Christ. Knowing people helps you to get beyond Terry's angry or hostile disposition, sensing that this is a person who is needy, frightened, and insecure. As he maneuvers to change the subject you are not distracted. You feel comfortable bringing the focus back to the subject-at-hand and challenging him there. While not being able to develop an intimate relationship with Terry, your authenticity as a witness for Christ will have a powerful and lasting impact on his life.

Endnotes

1. J. I. Packer, *Knowing God* (Downers Grove, IL: InterVarsity, 1973), 29.

2. Packer believes that as orthodox evangelicals we ought to "face ourselves at this point." Clarifying he wrote, "we can state the gospel clearly, and can smell unsound doctrine a mile away . . . . Yet the gaiety, goodness, and unfetteredness of spirit which are the marks of those who have known God are rare among us . . . . A little knowledge of God is worth more than a great deal of knowledge about Him." Ibid., 21.

3. Ibid., 21-22.

4. Note the words of Jer. 9:23-24 (TLB). The Lord says, "Let not the wise man bask in his wisdom, nor the mighty man in his might, nor the rich man in his riches. Let them boast in this alone: That they truly know me, and understand that I am the Lord of Justice and of righteousness whose love is steadfast; and that I love to be this way.

5. In *The Radiant Heart*, Costen J. Harrell emphasizes the process of character change by the Holy Spirit using Phil. 2:12, 13 [So you too, my friends, must be obedient, as always; even more, now that I am away, than when I was with you. You must work out your own salvation in fear and trembling; for it is God who works in you, inspiring both the will and the deed, for his own chosen purpose (NEB)]. In these verses "the Apostle is saying that in every sphere of life the Christian must take care that his conduct and character are shaped by the indwelling Spirit." The Spirit's influence should apply "to our pleasures, to work, to home, to politics, to church—to every question and duty that may arise." Costen J. Harrell, *The Radiant Heart* (Nashville: Cokesbury, 1936), 44-46.

6. You will recall the response of the woman at the well to Jesus as being different from any one else she had ever met.

7. Oswald Chambers, *My Utmost for His Highest* (Westwood, N.J.: Barbour, 1987), January 12.

8. Robert S. McGee, *The Search For Significance* (Houston: Rapha Publishing, 1990), xiii. Helpful resources on the topic of self include: Cecil G. Osborne, *The Art of Understanding Yourself* (Grand Rapids: Zondervan, 1967); John Bradshaw, *Healing The Shame That Binds You*

(Deerfield Beach, FL: Health Communications, 1988); Patricia Love, *The Emotional Incest Syndrome: What to Do When a Parent's Love Rules Your Life* (New York: Bantum Books, 1990); Kevin Leman and Randy Carlson, *Unlocking The Secrets Of Your Childhood Memories* (Nashville: Thomas Nelson, 1989); Larry Crabb, *Inside Out* (Colorado Springs: Navpress, 1984).

9. Harrell, 48.

10. The nature of spiritual gifts necessitates an attitude of selflessness and servitude. "Christian conduct and character are the *working out* of the indwelling spirit. By the fruits of one's life we may judge whether he is controlled and guided by the Spirit's prompting. (Read Gal. 5:19-26.)" Harrell, 46.

11. According to Ken Hemphill, spiritual gifts "provide the means for the believer to express love in the context of the community in terms of edification." Kenneth S. Hemphill, *Spiritual Gifts*, with a Foreword by Joel C. Gregory (Nashville: Broadman, 1988), 205. Hemphill asserts three necessary elements for a gift to be spiritual. First, it must be "a gracious gift of God, not an achievement of human will or an accident of birth." Second, believers will "surrender" their gifts willingly and unselfishly for the benefit of others. "Finally, the gifts will be used to bring edification to the community of believers." Ibid., 205-06.

12. Ibid., 277. For additional insight into the subject of Spiritual Gifts see also J. W. MacGorman, *The Gifts of the Spirit* (Nashville: Broadman, 1974). Many resources are available for helping persons to better understand how they are suited with gifts and passions for serving others. Bruce Bugbee, Don Cousins and Bill Hybels have collaborated to produce a workbook entitled *Network* (Grand Rapids: Zondervan, 1994). This study combines the passion, spiritual gifts, and personality of an individual with the objective of helping that person serve others in the most effective way in his or her most effective area of ministry.

13. "The original categories of personality division were conceived by a physician who was looking for a way to help his patients understand themselves and see how their emotional differences influenced their health.... The Taylor-Johnson Temperament Test and the Myers-Briggs Type Indicator, both long-standing psychological evaluations with universal credibility, provide expansions of the four original personali-

ties." Fred Littauer and Florence Littauer, *Get a Life Without the Strife* (Nashville: Thomas Nelson, 1993), 8. Additional sources for personality study include: David Keirsey and Marilyn Bates, *Please Understand Me*, 5th ed. (Del Mar, CA: Prometheus Nemesis, 1984); Tim LaHaye, *Transforming Your Temperament* (New York: Inspirational, 1991; and Keith Harary and Eileen Donahue, *Who Do You Think You Are?* (New York: HarperCollins, 1994).

14. Littauer and Littauer, 64.

15. Ibid., 7.

16. Ibid.

17. Ibid.

18. Ibid.

19. For a detailed discussion and explicit explanation of family diagraming by way of a genogram see: Monica McGoldrick and Randy Gerson, *Genograms in Family Assessment* (New York: W. W. Norton, 1985). Additional sources helpful in gaining a better understanding of family systems include the following: J. C. Wynn, *Family Therapy in Pastoral Ministry*, rev. ed. (New York: HarperCollins, 1991); Irene Goldberg and Herbert Goldberg, *Family Therapy: An Overview*, 3d ed. (Pacific Grove, CA: Brooks/Cole, 1991); Herbert Anderson and Robert Cotton Fite, *Becoming Married* (Louisville: Westminster/John Knox, 1993).

20. For a thorough study of alcoholism and its effects on the family see: Sara Hines Martin, *Healing for Adult Children of Alcoholics* (Nashville: Broadman Press, 1988).

21. For a thorough study of the nature and power of family systems theory see: Edwin H. Friedman, *Generation to Generation* (New York: Guilford, 1985); Friedman, *Friedman's Fables* (New York: Guilford, 1990).

22. 1 Pet. 3:15 (NIV).

23. Norman Geisler and Ron Brooks, *When Skeptics Ask* (Wheaton, IL: Victor Books, 1990).

24. Ibid., 10. Three reasons are given for pre-evangelism: unbelievers have good questions, Christians have good answers, and God commands it. Ibid., 11. Additional resources for facing critics include: Josh McDowell, *More Than a Carpenter* (Wheaton, IL: Tyndale House, 1977); McDowell, *Resurrection Factor* (San Bernadino, CA: Here's Life, 1989); Josh McDowell and Don Stewart, *Answers to Tough Questions Skeptics Ask About the Christian Faith* (Wheaton, IL: Tyndale House, 1980); McDowell and Stewart, *Reasons Skeptics Should Consider Christianity* (Wheaton, IL: Tyndale House, 1981); McDowell, *Evidence that Demands a Verdict*, vol. 1 (San Bernadino, CA: Here's Life, 1979); McDowell, *Evidence that Demands a Verdict*, vol. 2 (San Bernadino, CA: Here's Life, 1981).

25. C. W. Brister, *Pastoral Care in the Church*, 3d ed. (New York: HarperCollins, 1992), 54.

26. Ibid. See Gen. 1:26, 27; 2:7, 8.

27. Millard J. Erickson, *Christian Theology* (Grand Rapids: Baker Book House, 1985), 470.

28. Ibid., 471. Erickson, in describing the neediness of humankind, wrote, "Man cannot discover his real meaning by regarding himself and his happiness as the highest of all values, nor can he find happiness, fulfillment, or satisfaction by going out in search of it. His value has been conferred upon him by a higher source, and he is fulfilled only when serving and loving that higher being. It is then that satisfaction comes, as a by-product of commitment to God." Ibid.

29. Ibid.

30. For a psychological treatment of human beings from a holistic perspective, see Paul D. Meier, Frank B. Minirth, Frank B. Wichern, and Donald E. Ratcliff, *Introduction to Psychology and Counseling* 2d ed. (Grand Rapids: Baker Book House, 1991).

31. Brister, 56.

32. Ibid. Additional resources that lend insight into the human condition include: John Powell, *Why Am I Afraid to Tell You Who I Am?* (Niles, IL: Argus, 1969); Henri J. M. Nouwen, *The Wounded Healer* (New York:

Doubleday, 1972); M. Scott Peck, *People of the Lie* (New York: Simon and Schuster, 1983); Wayne E. Oates, *Behind the Masks* (Louisville: Westminster, 1987); David K. Switzer, *Pastoral Care Emergencies* (New York: Paulist, 1989).

Jimmy R. Sharp is a Ph.D. Student in Pastoral Ministries at Southwestern Baptist Theological Seminary, Fort Worth, Texas. He is in private practice as a pastoral counselor at Rapport Ministries.

PART TWO
Model Revival Sermons Blessed by God

CERTAINTY FOR AN UNCERTAIN WORLD

We live in a day that is filled with unrest. The only difference between now and the last time I made that statement is that now the unrest is just greater today than it was then. A great deal of the unrest in our world is brought about by chilling feelings of uncertainty. This is a terribly uncertain world.

I was in our Dallas/Fort Worth airport not long ago, and I was struck by the headline of a weekly news magazine that said, "Almost everybody in this country is unhappy." I knew it was the kind of headline they put on paper to sell the paper, but it worked on me. I bought one. I wanted to see if almost everyone in this country was unhappy. The article reported that there is more unhappiness in the United States today than there has ever been in history. It was a series of statements from people who supposedly were knowledgeable. One man from Georgia said, "People seem more upset and uneasy than at any time I can remember. The thing I hear them talking about all over the country," and he was a traveling man, "is this: that everything is so unstable and uncertain." It is always an uncertain age.

We have seen our dollar battered about abroad and watched the cost of living spiral upwards in this country. Most of us make more money than we've ever made, but it's not going as far as what we made ten or fifteen years ago. Economically, it's an uncertain world.

Internationally, it is an uncertain world. It was the "U.S. News and World Report" that suggested not long ago that there are forty wars going on in our world right now. Someone corrected the statement and said it is more like seventy wars. It is an uncertain world internationally. It appears to me that the world is seated on a powder keg and there are a lot of people running around with blow torches coming dangerously near.

Physically, it is an uncertain world. As far as your own condition, your life, it's an uncertain world. No one knows that he or she will be here tomorrow for sure. It is always an uncertain world. Physically, the world is chilled by haunting feelings of uncertainty. Things we once thought were nailed down are coming up all around us.

I want today to dare to speak to you, in an uncertain world, about certainty, "Certainty for an Uncertain World." A passage of Scripture that speaks of certainty is found in the little letter of I John 5:13. I suppose of all the verses in the Bible which have meant a great deal to me, there is none that has meant more to me than this one. "These things have I written unto you who believe on the name of the Son of God that you may know that you have eternal life." That you may *know*, that you may be sure, that you may be certain that you have eternal life. Here is a great word of certainty from God, "I've written to you who believe on the name of my Son that you may know that you have eternal life."

The first prayer I ever prayed was one I had committed to memory as a child: "Now I lay me down to sleep, I pray the Lord my soul to keep, if I should die before I wake, I pray the Lord my soul to take." It never occurred to me until I thought of this prayer with reference to my own children that one of the lines in this prayer contains a frightening prospect for some people. It is the line: "If I should die before I wake." Just suppose you should die tonight before you wake in the morning. What would happen to you? If you should join 150,000 other people in the experience of dying in the next twenty-four hours, where would you go? If you should die before you wake, will Jesus receive you unto Himself? Many psychologists tell us that one of the deepest yearnings in the spirit of man is the yearning for assurance or security. This is particularly true when it comes to things eternal or things spiritual. When it comes to what is going to happen to me when I die, I don't want any hazy question marks hanging over my head. This is something about which I want to know, about which I want to be sure. This passage of Scripture says "I've written these things to you who believe on the name of the Son of God that you may know that you have eternal life."

What I want to do is simple. I want to ask you three questions. I want to draw the answers to the questions from this passage of Scripture. Here is the first question: Is it totally possible to know that you have eternal life? Can you know beyond the shadow of a doubt that if you were to die today that heaven would be your home?

I know that there are people who say, "Listen, it is sheer presumption for you to say that you know that you have eternal life. You might hope so, you may think so, you may assume so, it might be maybe so, but you cannot know so." I submit to you that it is God Himself who says in this passage of Scripture that "I've written to you that you may *know* that you have eternal life." God says you can know that you have eternal life.

Somebody says that you'll never know for sure until you stand before God on the Judgment Day. I submit to you that it will be altogether too late to do anything about it then. God wants you to know that you have eternal life if your faith is in Jesus as your Savior. Not merely does He want you to know that in the sweet by and by, but also in the ugly, nasty here and now as well. I have thanked God many times that this passage of Scripture did not say, "I've written to you that you may *hope* that you have eternal life, or that you may *assume*, or that you may *wish*, or that you may *think*." I've thanked God that this passage of Scripture says, "I've written to you who put your faith in the Son of God that you may KNOW that you have eternal life. Is it possible to know that you have eternal life? God's answer to that question is "yes." I've written to you that you may know.

The second question is: Who among you can know for sure that he or she has eternal life? I quickly want to say that this is not a blanket coverage kind of promise. It is not written to all people everywhere; it is written to a select category of people; it is written to a particular group. "I've written these things to *you who believe* on the name of the Son of God." But what does it mean to believe on the name of the Son of God?

When our New Testament uses the word "belief," it might be translated "trust" or "put your faith in" or "commit yourself to." It is not referring to mere intellectual acceptance of facts. For years, I thought I believed on the Lord Jesus Christ because I believed everything about Him, but when the Bible tells you to believe on the Lord Jesus Christ, it is far more than merely believing *about* Him. It is more than intellectual faith. You can believe that Jesus was born of a virgin, that He lived a sinless life, that He was God, that He was flesh, that He died on a cross, was raised from the grave, and someday is coming again. You can believe all of that and still never really trust Him to be your Savior. The Bible uses the word "belief" as more than mere intellectual faith. It is more than merely trusting Jesus to do something for you in a temporal sense. I have asked people about their faith in Christ and they have said, "Oh, yes, I trust Him. When I was sick, I trusted Him to make me well." But merely trusting Him to make you well is *not* saving faith. I believe He wants us to pray to Him when we're sick. I believe He wants us to trust Him with illness. We will call that "healing faith." But "healing faith" is not saving faith. Some of you fly on airplanes a great deal. I fly almost once a week and I trust the Lord to take care of me when I'm flying. We'll call that "flying faith." I believe we ought to trust Him to take care of us, especially when it's overcast and ceiling and visibility are low.

Sometimes I forget to take the garbage out, and it's midnight, and I realize the next day is trash day. It's a long way from our front door to the curb at 12:00 at night. I take one sack in one hand and one sack in the other and make a mad dash to the curb and trust the Lord to take care of me while I make that trip. We'll call that "trash-carrying faith."

Well, you can have healing faith, you can have flying faith, and you can have trash-carrying faith and still not have saving faith. Saving faith is putting your trust in Jesus Christ to give you eternal life. It is trusting Him to forgive your sins. Has there been a time in your life when you put your trust in Jesus Christ to save you? This alone is saving faith.

I want you to notice that this passage of Scripture did not say, "I've written to all of you that are doing your best to be Christians that you may know that you have eternal life."

I asked a man not long ago if he were a Christian and he said, "Oh, I'm doing my best to be a Christian." Would you like to know how many people have become Christians by doing their best? Not a one. If you became a Christian just by doing your best, I want to tell you how good your best would have to be. The Bible says, "Be ye therefore perfect even as your Father in heaven is perfect." If you ever got to heaven by doing your best, there could not be one sin on your record, not one fault, not one mistake, not one error. If you're hoping to get to heaven by doing your best, I hope today that hope in you will be blasted because you will never get to heaven by doing your best. Your best simply is not good enough and there's not enough of it.

Sometimes we have a tendency to compare ourselves with other people. We look across the street at our neighbors and think, "I just know if it comes down to a contest between them and me, I'll get in before they get in." We look down the block a couple of houses and think, "There's not even a contest there." I want to tell you God does not grade on the curve. He doesn't say to you, "Look, if you make it up to this point, I'll let you in. But I'm going to cut the curve right here and below that point, tough luck." God doesn't say, "I'm writing to all of you who are trying to be Christians so that you may know that you have eternal life."

I talked to a man working on his car not long ago. I said, "Are you a Christian?" He said, "I'm trying to be a Christian." Would you like to know how many have become Christians by trying. This is going to surprise some of you, but you don't become a Christian until you stop trying and start trusting. You see, trying is self-effort. Trying says, "I believe if I worked hard until my fingers are blue to the bone, and I'm really red in the face, if I really try that hard, I believe God will save me." No, not because you've tried. You must come to Jesus Christ and say, "Jesus, I've tried and failed. I trust you to do it for me." That's the only way a person ever receives eternal life.

"I've written to you who believe on the name of the Son of God that you may know that you have eternal life." Has there ever been a time in your life when you put your trust in the One who died for you on the cross? Has there been a time when you nailed it down? Jesus, I trust you alone for eternal life. I put my trust in you to save me. If you can answer "yes" to that, I've got some good news for you. God says, "I've written to you who put your trust in Jesus, that you may know that you have eternal life."

Some of you say, "I really do trust in Jesus as my only Savior. But my faith is very small. I've never been able to shout along with the apostle Paul, `I know whom I have believed and am persuaded that He is able to keep what I've committed to Him against that day.' I'm more like the woman who has barely touched the hem of His garment. My faith is smaller than a grain of sand, smaller than a mustard seed. My faith is so small; it is wholly in Jesus who died for me. Will this small faith save me?" I want you never to forget what I'm about to say. It is not the size of your faith that saves you. It is the object of your faith, the Lord Jesus Christ who saves. Faith is not the Savior; Jesus is the Savior. Nowhere does God ever tell you to trust your faith. He tells you to put your faith in Jesus. I'm not asking you today how big is your faith. I'm asking you where *is* your faith for eternal life? Somebody in this building could have the greatest faith of anybody here and be lost forever. If your faith is in your own goodness, your faith is in your own keeping of ethical and moral standards. If your faith is in your church membership or your baptism, you can have the greatest faith of anybody here and not be saved. On the other hand, the smallest, most child-like faith in Jesus, the one who died for you on the cross, will save you eternally. I'm asking you today: Has there been a time in your life when you put your trust in the One who died for you?

There is a third question: How can you know for sure that you have eternal life? You say, "You're talking to me about eternal life. How can I know that I have that? It's outside the realm of my senses; I don't feel it with my fingertips; I don't see it with my eyes; I don't taste it with my tongue. How can I know I have eternal life?" You say, "I drove an old car into an automobile agency not along ago. I drove out with a new one. I know I have that new car. As I can look out in the driveway, the sunlight catches it. I get in it, and it even smells new. I put my foot on the accelerator and there's a surge of power. Three hundred-fifty dollars every month out of my checking account, I know I have that new car." Or you stood one day at the altar of a church like this. An officiating minister said, "Do you take this woman to be your wife?" You said, "I do." You know something happened, and you live with that relationship every day. But you say, "But you're talking to me about eternal life. I don't see that like I see my car; I don't touch that like I touch my wife or husband. How can I know I have eternal life?" Listen to the facts. "These things have I written unto you that believe on the name of the Son of God that you may know that you have eternal life."

Some of you have done what I did in the early months of my Christian life. You have rewritten this passage of Scripture. "These feelings do I give you on the inside that you may know that you have eternal life." Instead of looking to what He has written, you look instead to your feelings. We cannot depend on our feelings as to whether or not we have eternal life. Why? Our feelings are destined to change. Emotionally, we're so constituted that we don't feel today like we did yesterday. Sometimes I feel like I could go down to the Forest Park Zoo in Fort Worth, get in the cage with a tiger and fight him and whip him in three rounds. The next day I wouldn't want to tangle with a little kitten that kept me awake by crying on my window sill. That's the way our feelings are. They're up; they're down; they vacillate; they fluctuate; they oscillate. For you to depend on your feelings as to whether or not you have eternal life would be closely akin to trying to anchor a boat by casting the anchor on the deck. You have to anchor to something that is fixed and firm, that does not waver, that does not change, and that something is the infallible, inspired, inerrant, and you can pile those adjectives as high as you want, but this Word that God has given us--this is that in which we put our trust. His promise-- it does not fluctuate; it does not change; it does not vacillate; it does not oscillate. God does not say, "I'm giving you certain feelings that you may know." He says, "I'm putting it down in black and white. I am going on record. I'm going to say to you in my Word that you may know that you have eternal life if you put your trust in the Lord Jesus Christ.

I was saved when I was nineteen years of age. It was a pity I did not do it when I was nine. I would have if only somebody had showed me how. At nineteen I trusted in Jesus, but I began to question, "Am I really saved? Do I really have eternal life?" That question plunged me into doubt, and I lived in a valley of doubt for a number of months. If you had seen me, I would have been kneeling on the floor of my dormitory room in college, praying, "Oh Lord Jesus, I pray that you will save me. I trust you as my Savior; please save me." If I could have just seen His hand writing my name in the Lamb's Book of Life, that probably would have satisfied me for a while, or a special delivery letter, postmarked Heaven, saying: "Dear Roy, you're saved; signed, God;" that might have done it for a while. But God wanted to get me to the place where I was willing to trust in His promise, plus nothing. Oh, I praise Him for leading me to this promise in I John 5:13.

"I've written to you who believe, who trust Jesus, that you may know that you have eternal life."

I know if I died today that Heaven would be my home; I know that I would go to be with Jesus. I know it because I have the Word of a God who cannot lie. He says, I've written to tell you that you may have eternal life and know it, if your trust is in the One who died for you on the cross." When I die, I'm going to meet God, resting on the strength of His promise, saved by the blood of the One who died for me, assured by the Word of the God who did it all. If I should die before I wake . .

As it is with you right now, if you should die before you wake, would it be eternal life or eternal death for you?

Roy J. Fish is Distinguished Professor of Evangelism at Southwestern Baptist Theological Seminary in Fort Worth, Texas and occupant of the L.R. Scarborough Chair of Evangelism.

LIFE'S SUPREME QUESTION

People live beneath a row of question marks about God. Questions can become barriers, or they can open doors. Some people have the idea that we should never question God, but this is not God's idea. God is always open to honest inquiry. It is dishonest inquiry that God detests. Our questions are not going to confuse God. They are not going to shock God. He is always open to honest inspection. God is not trying to hide. He has gone to unbelievable lengths to make Himself known. He is certainly not trying to hide Himself from us. If you do not know Jesus as your personal Savior, it is not because God has deliberately hidden Himself from you. It is because you have not approached Him in honest inquiry. Honest questions indicate a willingness to learn and respond to facts. If we have no questions, we will seek no answers.

Questions are not new. Job said, "O, that I knew where I might find Him!" The psalmist said, "Where is thy God?" The martyrs asked, "How long, O Lord, before you act?"

Elisha asked, "Where is the Lord God of Elijah?" Look at II Kings 2:9-14:

"And it came to pass, when they were gone over, that Elijah said unto Elisha, Ask what I shall do for thee, before I be taken away from thee. And Elisha said, I pray thee, let a double portion of thy spirit be upon me.

And he said, Thou hast asked a hard thing: nevertheless, if thou see me when I am taken from thee, it shall be so unto thee; but if not, it shall not be so.

And it came to pass, as they still went on, and talked, that, behold, there appeared a chariot of fire, and parted them both asunder; and Elijah went up by a whirlwind into heaven.

And Elisha saw it, and he cried, My father, my father, the chariot of Israel, and the horsemen thereof. And he saw him no more: and he took hold of his own clothes, and rent them in two pieces.

He took up also the mantle of Elijah that fell from him, and went back, and stood by the bank of Jordan;

And he took the mantle of Elijah that fell from him, and smote the waters, and said, Where is the Lord God of Elijah? and when he also had smitten the waters, they parted hither and thither: and Elisha went over.

This is a crucial time in Elisha's life. As he stands on the banks of the Jordan, Elisha seems to ask, "Although I have Elijah's mantle, I still need his power." "Although I now have his office, I still need his power." "Although I hold his position, it is nothing without power."

"Symbols are nothing! Positions are nothing without God! Where is the Lord God
of Elijah?"

"The same God Elijah had, I must have. The same power Elijah had, I must have. The same fellowship with God Elijah had, I must have. Where is the Lord God of Elijah?"

Elisha confesses that power does not come from liturgy. It does not come from form. It does not come from activities. It does not come from wishing or wanting. It comes from God. "Where is the Lord God of Elijah?"

Sunday School teacher, herein is your power!

Deacon, herein is your power!

Christian, herein is your power!

Elisha was not asking to be a copy of Elijah. He was asking in order to be a voice for God.

In the last hours of Elijah on earth, Elijah asked Elisha, "Ask me what you want me to do. Can I do something for you?"

What shall Elisha ask for? Fame! Fortune! Wisdom! Position! What?

Just one thing, "I want a double portion of your spirit."

What was that spirit? It was an unwavering faith in God. It was an unhindered walk with God. More than anything else, Elisha wanted an unhindered fellowship with God.

Above the noise of Ahab and Jezebel, Elijah had proclaimed, "What does it matter what these say, `I see God high and lifted up.'"

Elisha was asking for an unwavering faith, an unhesitating obedience to God. There is no substitute for obedience. We will never experience the regal presence of God without obedience. We will never experience the joy of fellowship, the victory of living, the fruitfulness of service without obedience. Life is a shipwreck without obedience. We may want a thousand things in life, but the supreme need is obedience to God. He is Lord. A Lord is to be followed, served, and obeyed.

Elisha said, "I want a double portion of your unwavering faith and unhesitating obedience." As he stands on the eastern banks of the Jordan and cries out, "Where is the Lord God of Elijah?" he declares, "I want faith. I want obedience."

This is the greatest desire of the heart, the greatest discovery of the mind. This is life's greatest adventure--to know God and to be obedient to Him.

There are three pegs upon which we can hang our thoughts as we answer life's supreme questions, "Where is the Lord God of Elijah?"

This Is the Declaration of the Existence of God.

Any question about God starts with His existence. If Elisha did not believe in the existence of God, he would never had asked for Him. This was Elisha's declaration of the existence of God. So many times, we ask, "Where is God?" In times of tragedy and trial, we ask, "Where is God?" We have the faith as long as we see the fires fall. We have faith as long as we can ride on the crest of things going right. What about those times when nothing is going right? What about those times when there are no blessings? What about those times you are sitting by the side of the dried creeks of God's blessings? We are not to trust in the blessings of God; we are to trust in the God of the blessings. Some of you have gone through the crucible of life's furnace. It may be finances, loss of loved ones, broken health, severed relationships. If it could go wrong, it has gone wrong. We shout, "Where is God?" In times like those we want to ask Jesus, "Is there really a God?" What would Jesus say?

If we asked Jesus, "Tell us true, do we have a heavenly Father?" Would Jesus say, "No. We are orphans. We are homeless." Would Jesus say that. No! Never!

When we open the pages of the Bible, God's signature is on every page. When we examine creation, we discover that He has autographed every portion of his creative painting. God is alive and doing well on the planet earth. He has not declared bankruptcy. He has not filed for any chapter, regardless of the number. Believe it or not, God is not broke. He lived through the depression.

"Where is the Lord God of Elijah?" If we have those moments of doubt about God, it is not because God is off center. It is because we are. Our problem is that we want miracles. We want dramatic answers. We want a little fire from heaven, please. A little sky writing, God, just to let us know that You are still around. A little miracle, Lord!

There is nothing new in that. That is what Jesus faced constantly. Just a sign here! Just a miracle there! We do not live by signs or miracles. Signs are sight. We do not walk by sight. We walk by faith. Paul says to the Thessalonians that Satan can produce all of the signs and miracles that you want. The one thing that Satan can not counterfeit is faith. Hebrews 11:6 says, "Without faith, it is impossible to please God."

We are not to look for God in the spectacular, unusual, miraculous. If we do, we will miss Him altogether. God was not found in the flashing light. He was found in the darkness. He was not heard in the strong winds and raging storms. He is heard in the still small voice. "Where is the Lord God of Elijah?"

There are times when we wish God had a better Public Relations Department--a bigger advertising budget. If we were God, we would certainly do things differently. We would certainly put our signatures on every sunset, sign every tree, autograph every planet, and pen our names on every mountain. "Look what I have done!" Courtesy, God.

If we had the power to fling a few stars into space, we definitely would want our names on the committee that put them there.

God does not operate that way. God has done it all, but it is faith that acknowledges God as the grand architect and great building contractor. We do not elevate to go to God, God has already come to us. When we stop trying to go to God and trust God to come to us, we are flooded with His grace. We will not have to ask, "Where is God?" We will know exactly where He is. He will not be in the loud thunder of earth's roar. He will be in the silence that is so hushed that you will know God is present.

God does not jump at our every call. He does not answer the spiritual telephone every time it rings. There are times of silence. The silence of God is the test of our faith.

There are so many times that we go to God in prayer--nothing. "Well, I didn't expect anything, anyway." Some get mad at God. "Why, O God, don't you answer. I pray and pray and pray, and I get no answers. Why?"

We need to understand that God is not our servant. We are His. We are not His God. He is our God. If God answered the telephone every time we called, there would be no room for faith. There are times when God lets the phone ring, and He does not own an answering machine. There are times when God responds in silence to show us just how badly we want what we are asking for. It does not mean that God is not there. It means that we are not ready to talk. God does not want us to ramble. He wants us to get to the point.

"Where is the Lord God of Elijah?" This is a declaration of God's existence.

This Is the Desire to Experience God

Elisha asked for a double portion. Now he is ready to receive it. God is the God of experience. He does not operate on blind faith. Blind faith is no faith at all. He wants us to have experiential faith. Faith that does not experience God is no faith at all. There is no following without knowing.

There are some of you who do not know God. You do not know Him because you have never experienced Him. You have never experienced Him because you have not come to God on God's terms. You must come by faith. You must desire to experience God. God does not throw Himself at us. He offers Himself to us. He does not offer an escape from life. He offers the abundant living of life.

You must exchange ownership. You must trade in your title deed. He becomes Lord. You become a child. He becomes boss. You receive the blessing.

We want push button religion. Instant religion! We are like the lady looking at a new washing machine with a whole panel of buttons. As she looked at the machine, she asked, "Who do I get to push the buttons?"

We do not look upon God as One who is around just to get us out of trouble. We do not do as we please. We do as God pleases. "Where is the Lord God of Elijah?" We find Him when we desire to experience Him.

This Is a Demonstration of the Exhaustlessness of God.

Elisha stood on the Jordan banks with the mantle of Elijah in his hand. It was the same mantle. It was the same river. When Elijah and Elisha were leaving Jericho, Elijah struck the Jordan waters and the waters parted. Now Elisha stands, raises the cloak, and shouts, "Where is the Lord God of Elijah?" He struck the river and the waters parted.

"God, what you did for Elijah, I want you to do for me." God did.

God is inexhaustible in His love and mercy and grace. Just as He has transformed countless lives throughout history, He can transform your life. Just as God has transformed the lives of so many in this room, He can transform your life. Just as God has transformed my life, He can transform your life. The Bible says that God is the new beginning God. In 2 Corinthians 5:17, Paul says, "If any man be in Christ, he is a new creature; old things are past away. Behold, all things become new." Some of you have soiled the old page. You need a new one. I offer to you Jesus Christ. Some of you want desperately to start anew. I offer to you Jesus Christ. He does not remove the memories, but he does remove the guilt. He does not remove the scars, but He does heal the wounds.

You need the mantle of God's righteousness in your life. I offer to you Jesus Christ. You may have the mantle of machinery. You may have the mantle of position, popularity, honors, even religion. They are useless. Jesus is the answer. Jesus is not sitting in some heavenly grandstand looking down upon the playing field called earth. He is in the midst of life. He is parting waters. Right now, Jesus is ready, able, and willing to part barriers in your life--whatever they may be. He wants to have that unhindered relationship with you so much that He died on the cross for you and was raised from the dead so that you no longer have to live under a row of question marks about God. You no longer have to ask, "Where is God?" You will know that you know that you know He is dwelling in beauty and joy in your life.

In the garden, Adam did not search for God. Adam did not knock on God's door. Adam did not cry out, "Where are You, God?" It was God who cried out, "Where are you, Adam?" God did not hide from Adam. Adam hid from God. God is calling your name right now. He is in a hurry to do business with you. This is your divine appointment with God. Don't be late! Don't miss it! "Where is the Lord God of Elijah?" He is knocking at the door of your life. Wise is the person who opens the door and welcomes the King.

Malcolm McDow is Professor of Evangelism at Southwestern Baptist Theological Seminary, Fort Worth, Texas.

With Time on Our Minds

Can you remember when you had time on your hands? For some, it will take a memory stretch. While most of us no longer have the luxury of time on our hands, we do have time on our minds. Apparently, so did the writer of Ecclesiastes when he wrote these words:

> To everything there is a season,
> A time for every purpose under heaven:
> A time to be born,
>   And a time to die;
> A time to plant,
>   And a time to pluck what is planted;
> A time to kill,
>   And a time to heal;
> A time to break down,
>   And a time to build up;
> A time to weep,
>   And a time to laugh;
> A time to mourn,
>   And a time to dance;

A time to cast away stones,
And time to gather stones;
A time to embrace,
And a time to refrain from embracing;
A time to gain,
And a time to lose;
A time to keep,
And a time to throw away;
A time to tear,
And a time to sew;
A time to keep silence,
And a time to speak;
A time to love,
And a time to hate;
A time of war,
And a time of peace.

(Eccl. 3:1-8 NKJV)

In addition to these verses, the Bible has much to say about time. Today, I'd like to call your mind's attention to four of these facts. In the first place:

God Created Time As We Know It

With time on our minds, we are encouraged to look back to the beginning of time before time began when God created time. In those early hours and moments of time recorded in the first chapter of Genesis, God said, "Let there be lights in the firmament of the heavens to divide the day from the night; and let them be for signs and for seasons, and for days and years." (Genesis 1:14 NKJV). Time as we know it was created by God.

God began to place things into time and into space, and then created man and placed him in time as a subject of time to live in time.

Then Satan entered time. In his own way and in his own time he tempted mankind and man chose to follow Satan rather than follow God, thus disobeying God.

In that disobedience sin entered time, and God had to begin working within time to mold and shape a people to bring about the real purpose of time. God began to work first with all of mankind represented by that first creation, Adam and Eve. Upon their sinfulness and disobedience God began to narrow the focus of time, not to all of mankind but to a nation within mankind, the Hebrew nation. As God compressed time together, time became more full and the focus narrowed a little more to deal not just with a nation but with a family within that nation, the family of Abraham and Isaac and Jacob. As time went on, God narrowed the focus even more from all of mankind to a nation of mankind, to a family within that nation, to a line within that family, the line of David.

Finally, at the close of the Old Testament God had narrowed time down to a very narrow focus. The Old Testament closed with the line of David and the prophecy of One coming in that line who would fulfill all the purposes and plans of God for time.

In between the Testaments, whereas God was silent, God was not inactive, but working within the affairs of men and within time.

The Grecian people came to prominence and took over that part of the world known as the Holy Land. Even in their secular kind of experience and their secular kind of life-styles God used these people to bring about a language which would be for all to understand. By the time of Christ the world had the Greek language which was as close to a universal language as mankind had known since the early times of Genesis.

Then the Roman people came to power. Even in their secular kind of life-style God used that which they developed—the Roman road system-to enable the Apostle Paul to travel all over the world and travel in safety because Roman soldiers were everywhere. You don't have to be an advanced student of history to see God working in time, molding time, shaping time. Then one day:

God Sent Jesus In The Fullness Of Time

Like an hourglass God narrowed time down, compressing it together until finally Paul said it this way:

"When the fullness of the *time* had come, God sent forth His Son, born of a woman, born under the law, to redeem those who were under the law." (Galatians 4:4 NKJV).

In the fullness of time, when time could stand it no longer, when time was full to the brim, when time was stretching to express itself, when time was full and everything was just right, and all of mankind had been reduced to a narrow focus, GOD stepped into time again and brought forth the ONLY Son . . .

—born in a manger,
  —born of a virgin,
  —fulfilling the prophecies of old times,
  —raised in Nazareth,
  —ministering among Palestinians,
  —healing many without medicine,
  —helping people by the wayside,
  —saying over and over again to his followers, "My time has not yet come" (John 7:6).

They would come to him with a question and he would say, "My *time* has not yet come." The authorities would attack him severely, and he would say to his disciples, "It's alright—My *time* has not yet come." When he got ready to go to Jerusalem, they said, "You'd better not." He said, "Don't worry—They can't take me until my *time* comes."

One day his *time* came. They nailed him to a cross—stretched him out above the earth so that his time could come, so that the purpose as expressed by Paul in Galatians (that in the fullness of time God would send his Son to redeem the world) might take place. All of time created by God, worked in by God, shaped by God, molded by God, all of time—past, present, future — focused in on a skull-shaped hill where a man fulfilled the time and in so doing redeemed it.

The process of redemption, redeeming mankind unto God, is very similar to what we know of as redemption today. It was more popular a few years ago than it is now, but we used to save savings stamps—S&H Green Stamps, Texas Gold Stamps, all kinds of stamps. We collected them, put them in our stamp books, and looked in a catalog to see what we could purchase with those stamps. When we had enough stamps, we would go to a place that had a sign over the door that said "Redemption Center." We would go inside that building and trade in our valuable stamp books for something of greater value. We called that trade or process of exchange "redeeming the stamps." Redemption took place. That meant we had traded in one thing of value and had received something of greater or more significant value.

That's what God meant to do in time. With the only begotten Son, on the cross, God redeemed mankind. God Almighty "traded in" the Son as it were — one of value—in order to receive in return something of greater value—a risen Lord and a redeemed people.

Redemption took place. When the time was right, God redeemed mankind for all of time. Jesus came in the fullness of time, but the Bible also teaches:

God Will Someday Call Time

I would call your attention to this other idea, namely, one of these days God is going to call time. Listen to God's Word:

And the angel which I saw stand upon the sea and upon the earth lifted up his hand to heaven,

And sware by him that liveth forever and ever, who created heaven, and the things that therein are, and the earth, and the things that therein are, and the sea, and the things which are therein, that there should be *time* no longer. (Rev. 10:5-6 KJV)

One of these days God is going to call time. We sing, "The trumpet of the Lord shall sound and time shall be no more." All that we know of as time will cease to exist. God who created time and who worked in time and who sent the Son in the fullness of time is going to say, "Time's up, that's it, no more time." We can throw away our watches, throw away our datebooks, throw away our calendars, throw away our Daytimers, throw away our pocket computer diaries. We won't need them anymore. There won't be any such thing as time in heaven. It will be unending time—without beginning or end, eternal time. We won't have to worry anymore about being on time or saving time or keeping time or wasting time. There won't be anymore time. That which we know of as time will cease to exist when God says, "That's all the time there is."

A few years ago a popular song by Jim Croce suggested we could put, "Time in a Bottle". What a great idea—bottle up time for when we need it. Need time for family—uncork the bottle and let some family-time out. Need time for relaxation—uncork the bottle and let some free-time out. Within a year of recording the song, Jim Croce was killed in an airplane crash. Had he been able to bottle up time, the bottle would have been broken in the crash. Ultimately it is God and God alone, who calls time. Finally, the Bible teaches:

God—in the Meantime—
Wants Us to Redeem the Time

Consider this one other fact. God has a plan for us in the meantime, the time between the fullness of time and the redemptive work of Christ himself, and the time when the trumpet sounds and time shall be no more.

Listen to what Paul says to us, in the meantime, "See then that you walk circumspectly, not as fools but as wise, redeeming the *time* because the days are evil." (Eph. 5:15-16 NKJV)

The will of the Lord in the meantime is for us to redeem the time. That word means the same thing that it meant in Galatians when God said in the fullness of time the Son was sent to *redeem* mankind. The will of God for you and me as believers is to make good use of the time, to purchase up the time, to trade in time for better time.

So it is that when we come to profess our faith in Christ, we're saying in that action and in that commitment, "I give up all rights to my time. I give up future time. I trade it in. I redeem the time in order to get back from God new time, new birth, new man, a fresh start, a new beginning, a new season, a new time for a new start." We redeem the time, we buy it up, we purchase it from the Father—redeeming the time.

That's what Esther did. In the Old Testament Queen Esther was told by Mordecai the Jew, "That's why you're here." You see, Haman had built a scaffold on which to hang Mordecai the Jew as a disgrace to the Jewish people. Since Esther was the only one who could prevent the disgrace, the people came to Esther the queen to say to her, "Who knows whether you have come to the kingdom for such a *time* as this." (Esther 4:14 NKJV) Esther went to the king which could have cost her, her own life. She went saying, the time is right, and "if I perish, I perish!" Because she went to the king, it was not Mordecai who hung upon the scaffolds but Haman himself who hung upon those scaffolds—for the *time* was right. They indicated to Esther, that her place, her job, her assignment was right now—on time just like God planned.

Who knows but what *you* are here right now in a fullness of time because this is where God wants *you*. This is what God wants you to be about. It may be that you have been placed in the Kingdom of God for just such a time as right now. The longer I live the more I'm convinced that everything that happens in the will of God happens in a fullness of time. God has a way of molding and shaping our lives to bring about God's purpose within our lives. It just may be as specific as this—that YOU are here this day in a fullness of time so that God can bring about God's purpose and reveal God's will and redeem your time for the days ahead.

But we don't respond that way. We come before the Father sometimes and say, "Lord, I understand what you want me to do. I understand what you are saying. *Sometime* I'll do that. *Sometime*, I'll profess my faith in you. *Sometime*, Lord, I want to be faithful to a church. *Sometime*, Lord, I'm going to get around to placing my faith in you and joining a church. *Sometime*, Lord, I want to teach a Sunday School Class. *Sometime*, Lord, I want to be a part of the music ministry of the church. *Sometime*, Lord, I want to respond to your will. One of these days when the time is right, when I get around to it, *sometime* I'll do what I'm called to do."

Sometime may not arrive. This is the time that God has given. Today is the day that God has given. The time is growing late.

Leslie Weatherhead was pastor of City Temple in London for twenty-five years. In a book entitled, *Time for God*, Weatherhead mathematically calculated a schedule which compares a lifetime of "three score and ten" years with the hours of a single day from seven in the morning to eleven at night. It works this way:

If you are 15 years old, it is 10:25 a.m.
If you are 20 years old, it is 12:42 p.m.
If you are 30 years old, it is 1:51 p.m.
If you are 35 years old, it is 3:00 p.m.
If you are 40 years old, it is 4:08 p.m.
If you are 45 years old, it is 5:16 p.m.
If you are 50 years old, it is 6:25 p.m.
If you are 55 years old, it is 7:34 p.m.
If you are 60 years old, it is 8:42 p.m.
If you are 65 years old, it is 9:51 p.m.
If you are 70 years old, it is 11:00 p.m.

Whatever your age, time is rushing by. It's time to do what God wants you to do.

It's time for us to have done with lesser things and give heart and soul and mind and strength to serve the King of Kings.

It's time to tell the old, old story.

It's time to pray the Lord of the Harvest and get involved in the harvest.

It's time to weep o'er the erring one and lift up the fallen.

It's time to rescue the perishing and care for the dying.

It's time to break the bread of life and quit fighting over it.

It's time to reach out and touch without boxing gloves on.

It's time to send the Light instead of just building more expensive lighthouses.

It's time to stop designing new bait and get back to fishing for men.

It's time to stop analyzing the soil and get back to sowing seed.

It's time to help the loving Father call the prodigal home.

It's time to make home the kind of place where the prodigal wouldn't want to leave to start with.

It's time to turn our eyes on Jesus, to look full in His wonderful face so that the things of earth (the things of time) will grow strangely dim in the light of His glory and grace.

It's time! If not now, when? If not you, who? If not here, where? With time on our minds, it's time to respond.

Dan R. Crawford is Associate Professor of Evangelism and Missions and Director of Evangelism and Missions Practica at Southwestern Baptist Theological Seminary in Fort Worth, Texas. He is also occupant of the George W. Truett Chair of Ministry.

Five Steps to Servanthood

It was Bernard of Clairvaux who said, "The first virtue of Christians is humility. The second virtue of Christians is humility. The third virtue of Christians is humility. The fourth virtue of Christians is humility." If all of these four primary virtues are humility it goes without saying that humility must be an important facet of the development of the life of the servant. I want to suggest five steps for preparing our lives to be servants of Jesus Christ. You cannot arrive at that humility which is foundational to servanthood by trying to compare yourself with others who are more proud of themselves than you are. Nor should you try to contrive some "put down" of personal arrogance in the attempt to arrive at some superficial level of homemade humility. Rather, I want to encourage you to try to arrive at humility, not by striving to make yourself less than you think you are but to do it by simply comparing yourself with Jesus Christ.

I would like our text throughout this study to be Isaiah 6:1-5:

> In the year that King Uzziah died, I saw the
> Lord seated on a throne, high and exalted,
> and the train of his robe filled the temple.

> Above him were seraphs, each with six wings:
> With two wings they covered their faces, with
> two they covered their feet, and with two
> they were flying. And they were calling to
> one another:
> > "Holy, holy, holy is the Lord
> > > Almighty;
> > the whole earth is full of his
> > > glory."
> At the sound of their voices the doorposts
> and thresholds shook and the temple was filled
> with smoke. "Woe to me!" I cried. "I am
> ruined! For I am a man of unclean lips, and
> I live among a people of unclean lips, and
> my eyes have seen the King, the Lord Almighty." (NIV)

It is easy to see in this passage that Isaiah found his own comfortable humility level when he came face to face with the God who was "high and lifted up". In the face of the God who was "high and lifted up" Isaiah could readily say, "Woe is me, for I am a man of unclean lips and I live in the middle of a people of unclean lips."

Comparing yourself with Jesus Christ is not only impossible, it is unnecessary. You have but to see Christ and the comparison will strike you immediately. For when we see the pure white standard of anything utterly clean, we recognize that which is not. Sunlight, bright and pure, has but to fall on a dusty shelf to say immediately that the shelf needs attention.

Once you have arrived at the person of Jesus, you have but to stand next to his mile-high grandeur to notice that your own servanthood is dwarfed in comparison. Seeing him will work this wonderful effect that came to the prophet when he cried out that he was a "man of unclean lips."

Perhaps never in the history of Israel has there been a person who achieved as much as Isaiah. But all that he achieved begins with this public outcry of his own humility. In his humility we begin to see the God of great grace take effect and to magnify a life which probably never saw its true greatness because it was so fascinated with the greatness of God. Seeing Jesus Christ will, of course, work that same effect in your own life.

Let us then move to the five steps which will motivate us to move toward servanthood. And as we regard each one of these steps let us ask ourselves, "How can we officially do all that's required to reach these succeeding levels of our five steps toward servanthood.

Emptying the Self

Emptying the self is a process referred to in Philippians 2:7 as the *Kenosis*. *Kenosis* is the Greek word that implied *emptying*.

> Your attitude should be the same as that of
> Christ Jesus: Who, being in very nature God,
> did not consider equality with God something
> to be grasped, but made himself nothing,
> taking the very nature of a servant, being
> made in human likeness. And being found in
> appearance as a man . . . (Phil. 2:5-8 NIV).

To have the mind of Christ means that our minds will have to be focused on discipleship in ways that demand our own humility. This humility will come to us rather readily when we begin to understand that the whole process of incarnation described so beautifully in Philippians Two is merely a process of emptying ourselves.

There are a lot of things which we must get out of our lives: things like self-serving and self-importance. We may understand this emptying or "Kenotic" in this word picture. We may send a bucket down into a well and receive it back at the surface of the well as the rope retreats around the windless. But when the bucket has reached the top of the well, it will be full of water in direct proportion to the emptiness of the bucket when we sent it down. If, on the other hand, we send a bucket to the bottom of the well full of garbage, trash or rocks it will not come back full of water. It will come back partly filled with water and partly filled with trash and rocks. But if we remove the trash and rocks it will come back brim full of clean, pure water. The first step to servanthood is being sure we understand the process of emptying. It was the great poet, T.E. Brown, who said,

> If thou could empty all thy self of self,
> Like to a shell dishabited,
> Then might he find thee on the ocean shelf

> and say,
> 'This is not dead and fill you with himself
>   instead.'
> But you are so filled up with very you,
> And have such shrewd activity,
> That when he comes he says, 'This is enough
>   unto itself,
> T'were better let it be,
> It is so small and full,
> There is no room for me.'

It is in this process of emptying that we take the first step to servanthood. For there has never been a servant filled with ego, pride and arrogance who did not know the magic of the word Kenosis. It is in the emptying of all which is most offensive that we become most receptive to all that is most of blessing.

Applying the Rule of Christ's Increase

Applying the rule of Christ's increase is something that John the Baptist does in John the third chapter beginning with verses 27-30. When Jesus came on the human scene, John the Baptist began quickly to realize that his whole ministry of forerunner was over. He would soon be incarcerated in prison and killed. But he also realized he had done his life's work in introducing Jesus; he had prepared the world for the Kingdom of God.

As others of the Apostles began to follow Jesus, one can see that John might have owned a natural case of resentment, thinking 'why are my disciples following Jesus when they're my disciples and not his?'

> To this John replied, "A man can receive only
> what is given him from heaven. You yourselves
> can testify that I said, 'I am not the Christ
> but am sent ahead of him.' The bride belongs
> to the bridegroom. The friend who attends the
> bridegroom waits and listens for him, and is
> full of joy when he hears the bridegroom's
> voice. That joy is mine, and it is now complete.
> He must become greater; I must become less.
>   (John 3:27-30 NIV)

It is verse 30 that holds the marvelous glory and this second step toward servanthood. "He must increase and I must decrease" is the disciples meat and drink. Every servant of God must come to that place where he can legitimately say, "Jesus must be more and more as I become less and less. Unless we are willing to take this step of submission our own increase will continue to put our agenda first in our activities and schedules. We must claim this confession: "I lay by my agenda, my schedule, my hassled management of my life, that Christ may increase and I may decrease."

Surrendering Your Inadequacies

In this third step toward servanthood we surrender our inadequacies. All of us, of course, are overwhelmed by the fact that God not only saves us but gives us something to do as we take our place in His Kingdom. Who could ever feel worthy of being a personal servant to Holy God, the God of all ages, the God of Abraham, Isaac and Jacob, and especially the God who is the father of our Lord and Saviour Jesus Christ.

If you want to know just how intimidating Grace really is you must see Moses as he quails before God at the Burning Bush.

> Moses said to the Lord, "O Lord, I have never been eloquent, neither in the past nor since you have spoken to your servant. I am slow of speech and tongue."
>
> The Lord said to him, "Who gave man his mouth? Who makes him deaf or mute? Who gives him sight or makes him blind? Is it not I, the Lord? Now go; I will help you speak and will teach you what to say."
>
> But Moses said, "O Lord, please send someone else to do it."
>
> (Exodus 4:10-13 NIV)

Moses, like most of us, met God, awkwardly, first. In this fourth chapter of Exodus Moses does not immediately hide behind his inadequacies. He first meets God, who gives him several signs, like asking him to throw his rod down or put his hand in his bosom. His rod becomes a snake and his hand is afflicted with leprosy. There's no question, then, that God is the God of power.

What do we do when we come before the God of power? Moses-like we begin to make excuses. "God, I am not eloquent. Let somebody else. Send somebody else."

No great glory can come to our lives until we begin to surrender our inadequacies. God never calls the capable, only the available. We have but to measure and learn this glorious truth to lay aside our weaknesses and begin to revel in his glorious strengths.

It is wonderful to meditate upon Jesus as he sends his Apostles forth. He gives them instructions that in those days and times of trial, he will be with them. Even in those situations where we may not be victorious, he promises his presence. He says he will teach us in every hour of inadequacy exactly what we shall say (Luke 12:11).

So that the third step of learning to be a true servant of Jesus Christ means that we readily surrender our inadequacies.

Surrender Your Self-Will

As a fourth step to servanthood I want to encourage you to start each of your days in Gethsemane. And the place in which you must start is Matthew 26:42, when Jesus wrangled with his Father in Gethsemane over his tremulous, human fears of the cross:

> He went away a second time and prayed,
> "My Father, if it is not possible for this cup
> to be taken away unless I drink it,
> may your will be done.
> (Matthew 26:42 NIV)

One of the hardest confessions of our inadequacy (but an important step toward servanthood) is "Not my will, but your will be done." Until we can make such a surrender servanthood is all but impossible to us.

Most ministers and servants have faced their sense of calling with a great sense of inadequacy. In college dormitory rooms or perhaps at summer campground assemblies they once found themselves in Gethsemanes of their own creation, wrangling over whether their abilities were as great as God seemed to demand of them. But we must early learn that nothing much ever happens until we let go of our inadequacies and fears and confess, "Your will be done." How important it is to be able to make that statement.

I believe that the proper way to see our submission is to picture our own self-will being poured out even as we are made an offering unto God. Paul pictures, for instance, in Philippians 2:17-18, that our lives are nothing unless they are sanctified by God. Until we are so "sanctified", we will never become a "drink offering," poured out unto his glory.

> But even if I am being poured out like a
> drink offering on the sacrifice and
> service coming from your faith, I am glad
> and rejoice with all of you. So you too
> should be glad and rejoice with me.
> (Philippians 17-18 NIV)

Just Do It

The fifth and final step of submissive servanthood is very simple. Once we have made these four preparatory steps the fifth step is the step with which we actually begin to walk in his will. We must be honest. We may spend all of our life preparing to do the will of God and never really do it. But Colossians 3:23 is a verse that reminds us we must do all that we do in his name.

> Whatever you do, work at it with all your
> heart, as working for the Lord, not for men.
> (Colossians 3:23 NIV)

Be warned. Preparing to do the work of God can, in a sense, become a substitution for actually doing it. Which of us do not know people who spend a lot of time in prayer and devotion getting ready to do something for God that they never quite get around to doing. Their life is one long, endless, siege of preparation. Perhaps the Nike commercial is just right at this point, "Don't always be preparing. Just do it!"

Conclusion

I want to suggest these five steps to servanthood might be something that you could write out, scripture by scripture, on a large 5X8 note card. Take that 5X8 card and begin each day by practicing these five steps to prepare yourself for servanthood.

First, empty the self (Philippians 2:5-8). Second, apply the rule that Christ must increase and you must decrease (John 3:27-30). Third, surrender to God each morning those feelings of fear and inadequacy (Exodus 4:10-13). Fourth, submit your self-will as did Jesus in the Garden. Then your own agenda will be put beneath the feet of God's will (Matthew 26:42). And finally, number five, just do it (Colossians 3:23).

As you move each day on these five steps to servanthood, you must honestly claim them point by point, step by step as you move toward committed ministry. May God bless you as you learn the joy of servanthood.

Calvin Miller is Professor of Communication and Ministry Studies and Writer in Residence at Southwestern Baptist Theological Seminary in Fort Worth, Texas

The Missing Component

The Dallas Morning News recently had a three page spread on the origin of life. Throughout the story there was a reference to the missing component. I kept thinking, I know who the missing component is—The Creator.

Two-thirds of the evangelical churches in America are either plateaued or are in decline. In the Southern Baptist Convention one in seven churches had no baptisms last year. What seems to be missing? What is the missing component that has led to such malaise when there is such great need?

In Matthew's gospel there is a story about Jesus' ministry (Matt. 9:35-38) which may give us the answer to our quest to find the missing component.

And Jesus went about all the cities and villages, teaching in their synagogues, and preaching the gospel of the kingdom, and healing every sickness and every disease among the people.

But when he was with the multitudes, he was moved with compassion on them, because they fainted, and were scattered abroad, as sheep having no shepherd.

Then saith he unto his disciples, The harvest truly is plenteous, but the labourers are few;

Pray ye therefore the Lord of the harvest, that he will send forth labourers into his harvest. (Matthew 9:35-38 KJV).

As we read the story of Jesus' ministry as He went from village to village preaching the good news, we find that at the heart of the story is the word compassion. Jesus saw the people as sheep without a shepherd and felt compassion on them. Matthew frequently points us to the compassion of our Lord. In Matthew 14:14 Jesus was moved with compassion and He healed. In Matthew 15:32 He was moved with compassion and he fed the 4000. Matthew 20:29-34 tells us that He felt compassion and opened the eyes of the blind. Compassion will always find a way.

Since reading this passage I have been plagued with the question, "Why don't I have this level of compassion? Why don't our churches exhibit such compassion? How can we develop it?"

Jesus Understood the People's Condition.

Notice in the text He notes that the sheep were distressed and downcast. The disciples were perplexed by His description. They saw them as sheep, but they had not perceived the desperation of their condition. Do you understand the condition of sheep without a shepherd in Jesus' day? They were "bear bait." An unprotected sheep had a short life expectancy apart from the shepherd. Have you ever wondered why the shepherd with 100 sheep would leave the ninety-nine and seek for the one missing sheep? Why not leave him till the next morning? He knew that the sheep would never survive even a single night in the wilderness. Jesus saw the true condition of people. He knew they were dead in their trespasses and sin.

A few years ago I went to Alaska to preach in their state evangelism conference. Our meeting coincided with the salmon season. I'm not much of a fisherman, but they assured me that anyone could catch a fish when the salmon were running.

When I arrived at the bank of the stream, I could see why they were so optimistic about our fishing trip. You could see the fish as they swam upstream. This was fishing by sight and not by faith. You could stand on the bank and see the silvery shadows gliding past. With great excitement and anticipation I began to cast my lure. The fellow beside me was pulling in fish after fish. He soon caught his limit. I had caught nothing. I moved downstream into his position. Obviously I was not standing in the right place.

The longer I fished the more frustrated I became. It was getting late and I had caught nothing. I was desperate. I wasn't about to return home empty handed. I happened to notice a salmon in a shallow pool behind a rock near where I was standing. I noticed that he was barely moving and surmised that I could catch this fish with my bare hands. I called my friend and asked him to stand behind me on the bank. He asked me what I was intending to do and I told him I was going to scoop this fish out of the water with my hands and toss it to him on the bank.

"You can't do that," he asserted.

"Sure I can," I replied. "If a bear can do it, I know I can!"

"That's not the point," he exclaimed. "They will arrest you for doing that." He moved closer to the water seeing my determination to catch a fish. He glanced down at the salmon in question and declared, "You don't want this fish."

Thinking he was making light of its small size, I replied: "I don't care what size it is, I'm not leaving here without a fish."

"I'm not talking about its size. Look at this fish. You don't want this fish."

When I looked more closely I noticed that the dorsal fin was rather limp and a hunk of flesh was literally hanging from the side of the fish. "What's wrong with this fish?"

"It's dying," my friend noted. "Don't you understand, they are all dying. Once they begin to spawn, they begin the process of death."

"You're telling me these fish which are so successful at avoiding my hook are dying. The fish that are jumping up waterfalls are dying?"

"That's right! They may look healthy, but they are already in the process of decay."

Do you understand that people without Christ are dead in their sin? Do you really believe that they are eternally lost? Do you believe that your lost neighbor will spend eternity in hell? Do you witness like it? Without a clear understanding of the true condition of people, you will never have compassion.

Jesus Understood the Supernatural Power of the Gospel.

In Matthew 9 Jesus pointed his disciples to the bountiful nature of the harvest. The disciples must have found his reference to "fields ripe unto harvest" hard to comprehend. They had not seen much in the way of results. Jesus still had only a handful of followers and many ridiculed Him. The disciples could have pointed to the hard ground of the Pharisees and Sadducees. Yet Jesus promised them that the fields are ripe unto harvest. His words proved true as the Gospel soon penetrated hardened hearts and the preaching of the Gospel turned the world upside down. Jesus didn't look at His circumstances, He trusted in the supernatural power of the gospel.

We've been told that the boomers are turned off by theology, by the traditional church, choir robes, hymn books, and other assorted matters. We're not sure that the boomers are ripe unto harvest. We're not sure that the Gospel is powerful enough to reach our neighbor, our loved one. We are paralyzed because we've focused on the hardness of the soil. We've lost sight of the power of the Gospel.

Do you believe the Gospel is the power of God unto salvation as Romans 1:18 declares? Do you believe the Bible is like a two-edged sword? That it will not return void? Jeremiah compares the Word to fire and to a hammer that shatters rock (Jer. 23:29). Do you believe that? Now the harder question—do you witness like you believe these promises? If we are going to make a difference in our world, we must come to a healthy and balanced understanding of the supernatural power of God working through us. If you think you have inadequate resources to resolve problems, you will lack compassion to try.

I hear people object, "I just don't find it natural to witness." I respond, "You're not supposed to witness naturally, you're supposed to witness supernaturally." I am tired of people telling me they are trying to serve God in their poor, weak, humble little way. Stop it! God wants you to serve Him in His supernatural strength.

Jesus Understood the Significance of Prayer.

Did you notice the first instruction of our Lord to his disciples? No, He didn't, in the first instance, tell them to go into the highways and byways and compel them to come in. First, He told them to "beseech the Lord of the harvest to send out workers into His harvest" (9:38). Prayer is not only our vital link to heaven, it is the experience in which compassion is born. We cannot experience God in prayer without being touched by His compassion for a lost world. Notice too that Jesus made clear that the harvest was His. Evangelism is supernatural work, but we have been given supernatural resources. Why should God do anything apart from prayer that He has promised to do through prayer.

When I came to Southwestern Seminary, many told me that I faced an enormous, if not impossible, task. My first priority was to find someone to lead us in a prayer conference. I knew of T. W. Hunt's heart for prayer and his connection to our campus. I chased him by phone across the United States. God put it on his heart to come on short notice. I am convinced that what is happening today on our campus is the direct result of prayer.

Prayer is the cradle of compassion and the birthplace of supernatural empowering. People and churches that make a difference understand the significance of prayer.

Jesus Understood His Mission.

In verse 35 Matthew tells us that Jesus was going about all the cities and the villages, teaching, proclaiming the gospel and healing every kind of disease and sickness. Throughout His ministry Jesus was clear about and focused by His mission.

A telling illustration is found in the first chapter of Mark's gospel. Jesus had just healed Simon's mother-in-law and it had created quite a stir. Mark tells us that the entire city had gathered at the door (33). The next morning Jesus departed to a lonely place to pray. While he was gone the townspeople gathered in a great throng and His disciples came looking for Him. You can hear a note of reproach in Peter's voice as he stated: "Everyone is looking for You" (37). It is as if he were saying, "The church is full. Everyone in the city has gathered to see you. What are you doing in the wilderness?" Look at Jesus' answer. "Let us go somewhere else to the towns nearby, in order that I may preach there also; for that is what I came out for" (38). Jesus knew that His priority was the preaching of the gospel and, therefore, He could avoid those things that could so easily distract Him.

Do you understand the mission of the church? It has never changed! Our mission is to be obedient to Christ in the fulfillment of the Great Commission. We nod our heads in mental assent, but does our church budget and our corporate activity demonstrate that we understand that our mission is to make disciples of all the nations by going, baptizing, and teaching obedience to the Word of God? Yet only one in three Southern Baptist churches has any plan of outreach and one is seven baptizes no one in a given year. Yes we need revival!

Individually are your priorities the same as those exhibited by Jesus and commanded by Him? Are you going into the highways and byways and compelling them to come in? How long has it been since you told someone about your faith in Christ? How long since you invited a friend to church? Since you prayed with a neighbor?

Jesus Accepted Ownership for the Sheep.

The more I have thought about this passage, the more I am convinced that the key component in Jesus' compassion that is missing in ours is His willingness to accept ownership for the sheep. These were not just sheep without a shepherd. They were His sheep.

Do you remember the story of the prodigal son? The brother's lack of compassion can be clearly chronicled in the use of pronouns. The elder brother continually refers to the missing boy as his father's son. His father corrects him and underlines the fact that the prodigal was his brother.

Several years ago I moved to Atlanta for my work as the Director of the Southern Baptist Center for Church Growth. As part of the landscaping at our home, we put two small ponds in the backyard. These were to be the home for beautiful water plants and our Koi, a decorative fish.

I had barely finished construction on the pond and filled them with water when I had to leave on a church growth assignment. When I called home, my middle daughter Rachael answered the phone and excitedly asked if she could buy the fish and put them in the pond that day. I patiently explained to her that the pond had not had sufficient time to cure and, therefore, the fish wouldn't survive. She was unmoved by my careful explanation. She poured out all the emotional appeal of a 16-year-old daughter explaining how pretty the water looked and how her friends were coming over that weekend to see the fish. I finally relented, partially because I felt guilty for having to be on the road so much and partially because I am a push over when it comes to my girls. I did give her specific instructions to go to the discount store and buy five for a dollar gold fish.

When I called home the next evening Rachael wrestled the phone from her mom and squealed, "Daddy, I got the fish. You should see them, they are beautiful."

Somehow "beautiful" and five for a dollar didn't go together. I asked; "Rachael, you did get the goldfish at the local discount store didn't you?"

"Well daddy, I went there first, but the lady explained to me that I didn't want little gold fish for a pond. She said I needed Japanese Koi."

Needless to say Japanese Koi are not five for a dollar. At this point I knew it was too late to do anything other than pray. I arrived home several days later and Rachael and her younger sister Katie greeted me at the car. "Daddy come see our fish!" I was elated and surprised. Apparently the fish were still alive. They took me around to the pond and began to point out the fish and call them by name and identify each by owner. Each member of the family had their own fish. Getting into the spirit of things, I excitedly enquired about my fish. The girls pointed to a silver sardine-looking ugly fish. Seeing my disappointment they explained that the fish looked much better at the store.

That evening I began to notice that several of the fish were swimming erratically. Not a good sign. The next morning the first casualty had occurred. I found the girls at the breakfast table and informed them that one of the fish had died. In stereo they enquired, "Who's fish Daddy?" When I informed them that my fish had died, they casually returned to their eating and noted that it was no big deal since he was ugly anyway.

The fish continued to die with amazing regularity. As fortune would have it the last to die was the fish belonging to Rachael. The morning of his demise I walked into breakfast and she read the news on my face. She quickly asked, "Daddy, did my fish die?" When I responded affirmatively, she broke down and sobbed. At first I thought, "Wait a minute, it was no big deal when my fish died. Why are you crying now?" Suddenly it hit me, it doesn't really matter until your fish dies. The issue is ownership.

We will never see compassion restored to our churches until we are willing to accept ownership for the lost of our community. We will never personally reach the lost until we realize they are our personal responsibility. Who has God placed on your heart and mind this week who is lost? What are you willing to do about it? True revival will lead us to compassionate ownership of the lost.

Ken S. Hemphill is President of Southwestern Baptist Theological Seminary in Fort Worth, Texas and also serves as Professor of Evangelism and Church Growth.

REVIVAL BIBLIOGRAPHY

Avant, John, Malcolm McDow, and Alvin Reid, eds. *Revival: The Story of the Current Awakening in Brownwood, Fort Worth, Wheaton, and Beyond.* Nashville: Broadman and Homan, 1996.

Autrey, C.E. *Revivals of the Old Testament.* Grand Rapids: Zondervan Publishing House, 1960.

Baker, Ernest. *The Revivals of the Bible.* London: Kingsgate Press, 1906.

Bonar, Horatius. *True Revivals and the Men God Uses.* London: Evangelical Press, ND.

Cathey, Bill V. *A New Day in Church Revival.* Nashville: Broadman Press, 1984.

Criscoe, Arthur H. & Leonard Sanderson. *Decision Time: Commitment Counseling.* Nashville: Baptist Sunday School Board, 1987.

Davies, W. Elwyn. *As Eagles Fly: A Study in Revival.* Brooklyn: Bible Christian Union, 1971.

Drummond, Lewis A. *Spiritual Awakening: God's Divine Work.* Atlanta: Home Mission Board, SBC, 1985.

———. *The Awakening That Must Come.* Nashville: Broadman Press, 1978.

Edwards, Brian H. *Revival: A People Saturated with God.* Evangelical Press.

Finney, Charles Grandison. *Finney On Revival* (arranged by E. E. Shelhamer). Minneapolis: Bethany House Publishers.

Fish, Roy J. *Giving A Good Invitation.* Nashville: Broadman Press, 1974.

Hawkins, O.S., and Jack Taylor. *When Revival Comes.* Nashville: Broadman Press, ND.

Hawkins, O.S. *After Revival Comes.* Nashville: Broadman Press, 1981.

———. *Revive Us Again.* Nashville: Broadman Press, 1990.

Home Mission Board, SBC. *Revival Training Seminar Notebook.* Atlanta: Home Mission Board, SBC, 1981.

Huston, Sterling W. *Crusade Evangelism in the Local Church.* Minneapolis: World Wide Publishers, 1984.

Lloyd-Jones, Martyn. *Revival.* Westchester, IL: Crossway Books, 1987.

Murray, Andrew. *Revival.* Minneapolis: Bethany House Publishers, 1990.

Perry, Lloyd M., and John R. Strubhar. *Evangelistic Preaching.* Chicago: Moody Press, 1979.

Ravenhill, Leonard. *Revival God's Way.* Minneapolis: Bethany House Publishers, 1986.

———. *Revival Praying.* Minneapolis: Bethany House Publishers, 1984.

———. *Why Revival Tarries.* Minneapolis: Bethany House Publishers, 1959.

Rendall, Ted S. *Fire in the Church.* Chicago: Moody Press, 1974.

Richard Owen Roberts. *Revival.* Wheaton: Tyndale House Publishers, 1983.

Sangster, W.E. *Revival: The Need and the Way.* London: Epworth Press, 1957.

Short, Robert. *Evangelistic Preaching.* Nashville: Tidings, 1946.

Stanfield, V.L. *Effective Evangelistic Preaching.* Grand Rapids: Baker Book House, 1965.

Strack, Jay, and Robert G. Witty. *Do the Work of an Evangelist.* Nashville: Broadman Press, 1990.

_____. *New Testament Way to Revival.* Nashville: Broadman Press, 1989.

Street, R. Alan. *The Effective Invitation.* Old Tappan, NJ: Fleming H. Revell (Power Books), 1984.

Walker, Alan. *Revival Preaching.* Grand Rapids: Francis Asbury Press, 1983.

Wallis, Arthur. *In the Day of Thy Power:* The Scriptural Principles of Revival. London: Christian Literature Crusade, 1956.

_____. *Revival: The Rain From Heaven.* Old Tappan, NJ: Fleming H. Revell (Power Books), 1979.

Wallis, Charles L., ed. *88 Evangelistic Sermons.* New York: Harper & Row, 1964.

Webb, Aquilla. *Three Hundred Evangelistic Sermon Outlines.* New York: Harper & Row, 1924.

Whitesell, F.D. *65 Ways to Give Evangelistic Invitations.* Grand Rapids: Kregel Publications, 1984.

Cassette Tapes

"Evangelistic Preaching: A Self-Study Course in Creating and Presenting Messages That Call People to Jesus Christ." The Institute of Evangelism, Billy Graham Center, Minneapolis, Minnesota, 1990.